ROME AND HER KINGS

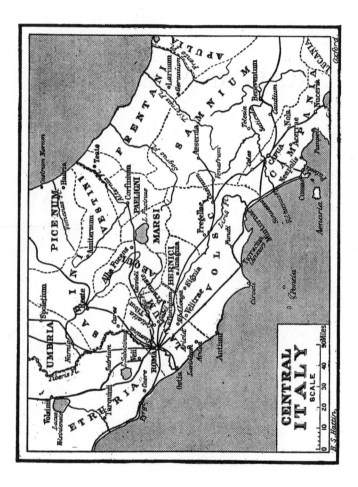

ROME
AND HER KINGS

EXTRACTS FROM LIVY I

EDITED WITH NOTES, VOCABULARIES AND
ENGLISH EXERCISES

BY

W. D. LOWE, Litt. D., M.A.

AND

C. E. FREEMAN, M.A.

BOLCHAZY-CARDUCCI PUBLISHERS, Inc.
CHICAGO, 1984

Cover by Leon Danilovics

Reprint of the Edition
Oxford at the Clarendon Press 1920

Bolchazy-Carducci Publishers, Inc.
8 S. Michigan Ave.
Chicago, IL 60603

Printed in the United States of America
International Standard Book Number
0-86516-000-7

PREFACE

This textbook is a graded elementary reader, consisting of connected excerpts from Livy I.

It is recommended as a reader to students who have had the basic introductory sequence of Latin.

This graded reader is followed by such standard tools as:

- Notes.
- Vocabulary of Proper Names.
- Latin-English Vocabulary.
- English-Latin Vocabulary.
- Exercises A and B.
- Recapitulating Exercises.
- Maps.

These tools were designed by W.D. Lowe and C.E. Freeman in order to: help the student make better and more stimulating progress in reading Latin; reinforce students' knowledge of Latin grammar and syntax; give them an opportunity to engage in creative composition of Latin sentences; provide sufficient background for the enjoyment and appreciation of the fascinating content in Livy I and his art as a writer, story teller, and historian.

As a Latin teacher I endorse the textbook. As a publisher I am proud of the privilege and the opportunity given to me to reprint this edition and thus extend the lifetime of a book that is well done and characterized by sound principles of methodology.

Chicago, 1979   Ladislaus J. Bolchazy, Ph.D.

CONTENTS

MAPS

HISTORICAL INTRODUCTION

Titus Livius, the poet-prose historian of Rome, was born at Padua in 59 B. C. He was probably of good family and well-to-do. Early in his life he came to Rome and spent most of his life there. He was soon admitted, because of his recognized ability in writing, to friendly terms with the emperor Augustus and the literary circle of Maecenas, Virgil, and Horace. Though of republican tendencies he held aloof from politics and spent most of his time in writing. His huge work, the history of Rome in one hundred and forty-two books, occupied him for forty years, until his death in A. D. 17. Only a portion of Livy's history remains as he wrote it; the rest is in an abridged form.

Livy was not a critical historian; his object was to tell the story of Rome as vividly and impressively as possible, to stir up interest and stimulate patriotism in his readers. We therefore find many inaccuracies and many prejudices in favour of Rome, many injustices against her enemies. He was not inclined to take trouble in sifting evidence and examining documents or statements of previous historians in order to arrive at the truth. He was content to take the view that flattered his vanity as a Roman or that pleased his dramatic sense as an artist. It is to the latter quality that he owes his fame and popularity, for his skill in graphic word-painting, his enthusiasm for great crises, his purity of language and brilliancy of style, at once put him far ahead of all his predecessors in the writing of history.

The method of writing history in the past was to chronicle events as they happened year by year during the office of the consuls for the time ; these yearly records were called *Annales (annus)* : or to write a memoir or biography of some distinguished general or statesman. Neither of these two types treated history or the record of a nation's life as a continuous whole. Livy took as his central thread the greatness of Rome and wove his noble work round it. Such was the reputation that he won even in his lifetime that the story is told of a Spaniard who came all the way from Cadiz to Rome simply to see Livy and, when he had done so, returned home at once without even considering the other glories of Rome.

It must be remembered in reading these stories that when the Gauls captured and burned Rome in 390 B.C. they destroyed most of the old records which were stored in the Capitol, and that therefore the accounts of events preceding this date are most unreliable, and in many cases mere legends and inventions. These legends Livy records without examination or criticism : they pleased his romantic sense and animated his history. And it is this wealth of legend and mythology combined with his sense of romance and drama, set forth in true poetic diction, that makes his history of Rome a prose-epic.

ROME AND HER KINGS

[It may be taken as a general rule that final *-i, -o, -u,
-as, -es, -os,* and all monosyllables ending in a vowel are
long with the exception of *-ně, -quě, -vě.*]

I

*The destruction of Troy and the flight of the Trojans to
Italy, where Aeneas founds a new kingdom.*

Graeci cum Troiānīs bellum gessērunt ;
decimo anno Troiam cēpērunt.
Multi Troiāni ex Asiā effūgērunt,
post multos labōres in Ītaliam vēnērunt :
5   hōrum dux est Aenēas, fīlius Veneris.
    Ibĭ Troiāni ēgressi sunt, praedamque ex ăgrĭs
agēbant.
    Latīnus, rex illĭus terrae, cum Troiānīs manūs
conserēbat :
10   ab Aenēā proelio victus est, pācemque fēcit :
dēīnde fīliam Lāvīniam Aenēae in mātrimōnium
dedit.
    Troiāni oppidum condunt : Aenēas ab nōmine
uxōris Lāvīnium appellat.

II

The migration to Alba Longa: a succession of kings follows
until Numitor is driven out by Amulius, and his children
are killed.

Post mortem Aenēae Ascanius fīlius regnat. 15
Hic Lāvīnium, urbem opulentam, mātri relīquit ;
novam ipse aliam urbem sub Albāno monte
condidit :
huic oppido erat nōmen Alba Longa.
Mortuo Ascanio, regnat Silvius. 20
Post Silvium regnāvērunt multi rēges.
Tandem Procas rex factus est, pater Numitōris
atque Amūlii.
Numitōri, qui nātu maximus erat, regnum Procas
lēgat. 25
Mox tamen, pulso frātre, Amūlius regnat : addit
scelus sceleri.
Līberos frātris occīdit ; frātris fīliam, Rēam
Silviam, Vestālem lēgit.

III

Rea Silvia has twin sons: Amulius plans to destroy them,
but by a lucky fate they are saved and are nurtured
first by a wolf and then by Faustulus, the shepherd,
and his wife.

Rēae Silviae Martique deo, ut aiunt, gemini fīlii 30
erant.
Amūlius īrātus et perturbātus sacerdōtem vincīri
iubet,

puerosque in flūmen mitti.

35 Forte super rīpas Tiberis effūsus est :
itaque homines flūmen adīre non possunt.
Constituunt in proximīs stagnīs pueros expōnere.
Alveus, in quo pueri expositi erant, hūc illūc
fluitābat.

40 Mox tamen flūmen intrā rīpas recēdēbat,
et alveum in siccā rīpā destituit.
Deīnde lupa sitiens ex montibus flūmen adiit,
vāgītumque geminōrum audiit.
Lupa adiit, et pueros linguā lambens lacte aluit.

45 Lupam cum puerīs Faustulus, magister rēgii
pecoris, invēnit.
Hos domum Faustulus fert Lārentiaeque uxōri
dat.
Sīc gemini· a pastōribus ēducāti sunt.

IV

*Romulus and Remus grow up. Remus is captured by
robbers, and is in danger of death; Faustulus reveals
their birth. Romulus and Numitor plan and effect the
death of Amulius, and Numitor regains the kingdom.*

50 Rōmulus Remusque, iam iuvenes, in lātrōnes
impetum fēcērunt,
praedamque pastōribus dīvidunt.
Itaque lātrōnes, praedā āmissā, Remum insidiīs
cēpērunt, sed Rōmulus vi se dēfendit.

55 Lātrōnes Remum trahunt ad Amūlium : dīcunt
eum in Numitōris āgros impetum fēcisse.

Itaque Numitŏri ad supplicium Remus dēditur.

Ab initio Faustulo spes fuerat se ēducāre rēgiam stirpem,

nam expositos esse iussu rēgis infantes sciēbat : 60 itaque Rŏmulo rem aperit.

Numitor etiam Remum agnŏverat : parant consilium.

Rŏmulus, collectā pastŏrum manu, in regem impetum fecit, Remus cum amīcīs Numitŏris frā- 65 trem adiuvat.

Sīc Amūlium occīdunt, et Numitor regnum adipiscitur.

V

As the brothers were twins they resort to taking auguries to decide which of them is to found the new city. The omens are doubtful and a quarrel is the result. The accounts of Remus' death vary. Romulus founds and rules Rome.

Posteā Rŏmulus Remusque constituunt urbem condere in iīs locīs ubī expositi et ēducāti erant.   70

Quod gemini erant, incertum fuit uter nōmen novae urbi daret et regnāret.

Tandem statuērunt auguria capere.

Remus prior sex vultures vīdit, sed mox Rŏmulus duodecim.   75

Inde altercātio oritur, deinde rixa, quā in rixā Remus occīsus est.

Multi tamen narrant Remum novos mūros transiluisse, ut frātrem vexāret.

80 Tum Rōmulus, ut hi dīcunt, haec verba locūtus
est:
    ' sīc pereant omnes qui transilient moenia mea',
et statim frātrem interfēcit.
    Ita sōlus imperium Rōmulus adeptus est, et ur-
85 bem novam nōmine suo appellāvit.

VI

*Rōmulus, the new king, sets about enlarging his kingdom.
    One of the chief difficulties is the lack of wives for the
    Romans.   During some festal games the Romans seize
    wives from among the Sabine maidens.*

Rōmulus, creātus rex, duodecim lictōres sumpsit,
et iūra populo dedit.
    Interim urbs crescēbat et mūniēbātur.
    Rex asȳlum inter duos lūcos aperit:
90 ad hoc asȳlum omnes, līberīque et servi, qui
novārum rērum avidi erant, perfūgērunt.
    Praetereā centum creat senātōres, qui pātres
appellāti sunt.
    Hi senātōres Rōmulum monēbant ut lēgātos circā
95 vīcīnas gentes mitteret.
    Paucae enim fēminae in urbe erant.
    Nusquam benignē lēgātio audīta est: itaque
Rōmāni īrascēbantur.
    Mox multi Rōmam convēnēre qui novam urbem
100 vidēre volēbant.
    Inter lūdos, signo dato, Rōmāni virgines Sabī-
nōrum rapere incipiēbant: multae captae sunt.

Virgines hoc aegrē ferēbant, sed ipse Rōmulus
eas hortābātur ut sortem suam acciperent et
Romānīs nūberent :   105
  neque rēgis precibus diū resistēbant.

VII

*The Sabines and people of Caenina endeavour to recover their
daughters. The treachery and death of Tarpeia. In
the midst of the battle the Sabine women implore their
fathers and husbands to cease from fighting. Peace is
made.*

Mox Caenīnenses in ăgrum Rōmānum impetum
fēcērunt ut virgines reciperent.
  Sed Rōmulus fugat exercitum et rēgem occīdit.
  Sabīnī tamen dolum nectēbant.   110
  Spurius Tarpēius Rōmānae praeerat arci.
  Hūius fīliam, Tarpēīam, auro corrumpit Tatius,
rex Sabīnōrum, ut armātos in arcem accipiat.
  Sabīnī aureas armillas magni ponderis bracchio
laevo habēbant :   115
  Tarpēīa Tatio ita dixit : 'Sabīnī, arcem intrantes,
id mihī dent quod bracchio laevo habent.'
  Sed Sabīnī pro aureīs dōnīs scūta in eam coniē-
cērunt quae in sinistrīs manibus habēbant.
  Ita, scūtīs oppressa, Tarpēīa periit.   120
  Sabīnī igitur arcem tenuērunt ; et diē postero
cum Rōmānīs manūs conseruērunt.
  Sed Sabīnae mulieres inter tēla properābant et
pătres et viros ōrābant ne sanguine se maculārent.

125 Exclamābant enim se fīlias esse alterīus populi,
uxōres alterīus.

Ita pax est facta.

VIII

*The dual kingdom begins. After the death of Tatius,
Romulus reigns alone and Rome flourishes under his
rule. The sudden, unaccountable death of Romulus,
and rumours of his murder. The latter are silenced
by the miraculous appearance of Romulus and his
promise of glory for Rome.*

Aliquot annos erant duo rēges, Rōmulus et Tatius :
Tatio mortuo, Rōmulus sōlus regnābat.

130 Trecentos equites ad custōdiam corporis, quos
appellāvit Celeres, non in bello sōlum, sed etiam in
pāce habuit. Urbem adeo firmāvit et auxit ut
quādrāgintā annos tūtam pācem habēret.

Rōmulus recensēre exercitum in Campo consti-
135 tuit : subito coorta est tempestas cum magno fragōre
tonītribusque.

Rex denso nimbo est cēlātus et a conspectu amī-
cōrum raptus. Nec dēinde in terrīs Rōmulus fuit.

Rōmāni, tranquillā lūce redeunte, vacuam sēdem
140 rēgiam vīdērunt et crēdēbant Rōmulum ad caelum
raptum esse procellā.

Itaque multi Rōmulum, deum deo nātum, ad
caelum rediisse crēdidērunt.

Alii tamen putābant rēgem a pātribus esse inter-
145 fectum.

Brevi tempore Proculus senātor Rōmānus populo

haec nuntiāvit: ' Rōmulus ', inquit, ' Quirītos,
parens urbis hūius, hodiē, caelo dēlapsus, ad me
vēnit, et me hīs verbīs allocūtus est:

"abi, nuntiā Rōmānīs deos velle ut mea Rōma 150
caput orbis terrārum sit: proinde rem mīlitārem
colant ne ullae vīres armīs Rōmānīs resistere
possint"; haec locūtus ad caelum rediit.'

Hīs verbīs Proculi omnes crēdidērunt.

IX

*After Romulus' death, there was an interregnum, during
which a hundred senators ruled. Owing to the com-
plaints of the people, the Sabine, Numa Pompilius,
was elected king. He was a just and good man, and
gave law and order to the now strong and flourishing
city. He strengthened his authority by claiming divine
guidance.*

Rōmulo mortuo, incertum erat quis regnum 155
adipiscerētur.

Prīmo a centum patribus cīvitas administrābatur:
plebs tamen fremere et dīcere, centum dominos pro
ūno factos esse.

Tum interrex, cīvibus convocātīs, ' Quirītes ', 160
inquit, ' rēgem creāte: ita pătribus vīsum est.
Pătres dēinde comprobābunt, si dignum creāverītis.'

Tum plebs clāmāre et rogāre ut senātus dēcer-
neret quis Rōmam regeret.

Numa Pompilius, vir inclutā iustitiā, Sabīnus, 165
a pătribus rex creātus est.

Ut tamen deos consuleret, augurem vocavit, qui
sīc precātus est: 'Iuppiter, si est fas hunc Numam
Pompilium rēgem Rōmae esse, tu signa certa da.'
170 Quibus datīs, dēclārātus est rex Numa.

Regnum ita adeptus, Numa urbi ius, lēges, mōres
dare constituit.

Ut Rōmānīs persuādēret etiam deos hoc velle,
rex simulat se cum deā Ēgeriā noctu colloqui, et
175 deam de hīs rēbus se docēre.

Sācra instituit: sacerdōtes creāvit: annum in
duodecim menses ad cursūs lūnae dīvīsit: dies
nefastos fastosque fēcit.

Lūcus erat qui spēluncam fontemque habēbat.
180 Hunc locum Camēnīs Numa sācrāvit, quia ibī cum
deā Ēgeriā colloquēbātur.

Rōmulus septem et trīgintā regnāvit annos,
Numa tres et quādrāgintā. Iam Rōma aucta est
artibus et belli et pācis.

X

The warlike Tullus Hostilius succeeds Numa; he is afraid
that the Romans will become effeminate if peace is
prolonged, so he decides to fight against the Albani.
The Albani besiege Rome: Tullus makes a counter-
invasion into their territory. The two leaders agree
to settle the war by a contest between three champions
from each side.

185 Numā mortuo, ad interregnum res rediit. Tandem Tullum Hostīlium rēgem populus pātresque
creāvērunt.

Hic non sōlum proximo rēgi dissimilis erat, sed
etiam ferōcior quam Rōmulus. Arbitrātus cīvitātem ōtio senescere bellum gerere constituit.   190

Mox Albānīs bellum intulit. Albāni priōres
ingenti exercitu in ăgrum Rōmānum impetum
fēcērunt: castra prope Rōmam pōnunt, et urbem
fossā circumdant.

In hīs castrīs Cluilius, Albānus rex, moritur; 195
dictatōrem Albāni Mettium Fufetium creant.

Interim Tullus nocte infesto exercitu in ăgrum
Albānum iter fēcit. Statim Mettius, castrīs relictīs,
quam celerrimē hostem sequitur.

Ducibus congressīs placet sine multo sanguine 200
rem dēcernere.

Forte in duōbus exercitibus tum erant trīgemini
frātres: in Rōmāno exercitu tres Horātios, in
Albāno tres Curiātios fuisse ferunt.

Trīgeminos rex uterque rogat, ut pro suā pătriā 205
ferro dīmicent. Frātribus hoc placet.

Foedus ictum est inter Rōmānos et Albānos hīs
lēgibus, ut is populus, cūius prōpugnātores eo
certāmine vīcissent, alteri populo cum bonā pāce
imperāret.   210

XI

*The fight between the Horatii and Curiatii at first went
  badly for the Romans, but by cunning tactics the
  surviving Roman killed his three opponents.*

Foedere icto trīgemini arma capiunt et in medium
inter duas acies prōcēdunt.

Consēderant ŭtrimque pro castrīs duo exercitŭs.

Datur signum, infestīsque armīs iuvenes con-
215 currunt. Consertīs dēīnde manibus, duo Rōmāni
concidērunt, vulnerātī sunt tres Albāni.

Cum hoc vīdissent Albāni gaudio conclāmābant:
Rōmāni spem tōtam dēpōnēbant.

Rōmānus tamen, qui supererat, integer fuit. Ut
220 Albānos dissipāret, coepit fugam capessere.

Mox respiciens videt ūnum ex tribus haud procul
ab sēsē abesse: statim in eum magno impetu rediit:
dum Albānus exercitus Curiātiēs hortātur ut frātri
subveniant, Horātius, caeso hoste, victor secundam
225 pugnam petēbat.

Sic alterum Curiātium occīdit priusquam alter
consequi posset.

Iamque numerus ŭtrīmque par erat, sed nec spes
nec vīres pares.
230 Rōmānus enim ferro intactus, Albānus fessus
vulnere erat.

Rōmānus exsultans, ' duos ', inquit, ' frātrum
Mānibus dedi: tertium, ut Rōmānus Albāno imperet,
dabo.'
235 Tum ferro hostem occīdit: iacentem spoliat.

XII

On the return of the victor to Rome, his sister seeing the spoils of victory bewails the death of her destined husband, one of the Curiatii, and Horatius in a fit of indignation kills her. He is brought to judgement but is finally acquitted on the pathetic appeal of his father.

Exercitus inde domum rediit. Horātius inter prīmos ībat trīgemina spolia ferens.

Horātii soror, quae desponsa ūni ex Curiātiīs fuerat, victōrem ante portam urbis vīdit.

Cognitā veste sponsi quam frāter gerēbat, solvit 240 crīnes et flēbiliter nōmine sponsum mortuum appellat.

Frāter, in victōriā suā et publico gaudio, sorōri sīc querenti irātus est. Stricto itaque gladio puellam occīdit.   245

' Abi hinc ', inquit, ' ad sponsum, oblīta frātrum mortuōrum vīvīque, oblīta pătriae. Sic eat, quaecumque Rōmāna hostem lūgēbit.'

Prīmo hoc facinus pătribus plēbīque ătrox vidēbātur, et Horātius raptus est in iūs ad rēgem, qui, 250 concilio populi convocato, lictōrem iussit manūs Horātii colligāre.

Accesserat lictor manūsque colligābat, sed Horātius, ' prōvoco ', inquit. Itaque prōvocātiōne certātum ad populum est.   255

Tum Publius Horātius pater clāmāvit se iūdicāre

fīliam suam iūre caesam esse ; mox ipsum iuvenem
est amplexus, spolia Curiātiōrum ostentans. Deīnde
populum ōrābat ne se orbum līberīs faceret.
260   Tandem populus Herātium absolvit magis admī-
rātiōne virtūtis quam iūre causae.

XIII

*The people of Alba are transferred to Rome and help to
strengthen the Roman army. Tullus defeats the Sabines.
Ominous portents are announced and are soon followed
by a pestilence. Tullus endeavours to appease the Gods
but is struck by lightning and destroyed.*

Posteā equites praemissi sunt Albam, qui multitūdinem Rōmam trādūcerent : legiōnes deīnde
ductae ad dīruendam urbem sunt.
265   Ita Roma crescit Albae ruīnīs : dūplicātur cīvium
numerus.
Equitum decem turmas ex Albānīs Tullus lēgit,
et legiōnes novas conscripsit.
Tum Tullus Sabīnīs bellum indīcit, genti opulen-
270 tissimae.
Pugna ātrox fuit, sed Rōmāni peditum rōbore et
equitātu iam plūrimum valēbant. Tandem equites
ordines Sabīnōrum turbāvērunt. Hostes fugerunt
et permulti occīsi sunt.
275   Paulo post nuntiātum est rēgi pātribusque in
monte Albāno lapidibus plūvisse : etiam vōcem

ingentem ex summi montis lūco esse audītam, ut
sācra Albāni facerent.

Mox pestilentia incidit in urbem : prīmo bellicōsus rex nullam ab armīs quiētem dedit, crēdēbat 280
enim suos salūbriōres futūros esse mīlitiae quam
domi. Tandem ipse quoque morbo est implicitus.

Tum rēgem trādunt volvisse commentārios
Numae, et ibī occulta sācrificia Iovi facta invēnisse.

Tullus dīcitur haec sācrificia fēcisse. Iuppiter 285
tamen, īrātus rēgi, Tullum cum domo fulmine
percussit.

Tullus · Hostīlius magnā glōriā belli regnāvit
annos duos et trīgintā.

XIV

*Ancus Martius succeeded Tullus : he defeated the Latins
who presumed on his supposed weakness of character.
He proceeded to enlarge and strengthen Rome. Lucumo
(the future Tarquinius Priscus) emigrates from Tarquinii
to Rome. He is welcomed by very favourable omens.*

Mortuo Tullo, Ancus Martius rex creatus est. 290
Numae nepos erat, filiā ortus.

Mox Latīni, cum quibus, Tullo regnante, ictum
foedus erat, incursiōnem in āgrum Rōmānum
fēcērunt.

Ancus, tantā hostium iniūriā incensus, cum res 295
frustrā repetiisset, lēgātum mīsit, qui bellum Latīnis

indīceret. Is postquam ad locum pervēnit, hastam
in fīnes eōrum coniēcit. Hoc modo tum bellum
indīcēbātur.

300 Ancus, cūrā sācrōrum sacerdōtibus mandātā,
exercitu conscripto, profectus in hostes, vi cēpit
urbem Latīnōrum, et multitūdinem omnem Rōmam
trāduxit, cui Aventīnum datum est.

Iāniculum quoque urbi adiēcit, non inopiā loci,
305 sed ne ea arx hostium esset. Id non sōlum mūro
sed etiam ponte urbi coniungere Anco placuit.

Anco regnante, Lucumo, vir dīves, Tarquiniīs—
nam ibi nātus erat—Rōmam vēnit cupīdine maximi
ac spe magni honōris.

310 Lucumōnem, hērēdem pātris, auxit Tanaquil
summo loco nāta, quam in matrimōnium duxerat.

Lucumo cum mīgrāre Tarquiniīs constituisset,
ad Iāniculum forte iter fecit. Ibī aquila ad eum
advolāvit et pīleum abstulit: cum magno clangōre
315 volitāvit, deīnde capiti pīleum reposuit: inde sub-
līmis abiit.

Tum Tanaquil, perīta prōdigiōrum, virum amplexa
iubet eum alta spērāre: aquilam enim vēnisse, dei
nuntium, ut faustum fātum portenderet. Has spes
320 sēcum portantes urbem ingressi sunt.

XV

*Lucumo takes the name of Tarquinius Priscus. He in-
gratiates himself with Ancus and is made guardian of
the king's sons. By a trick he succeeds Ancus on the
latter's death. He strengthens Rome and wishes to
increase the number of the centuries of knights. Attus,
the augur, persuades him against his will to refrain
from doing this, but the king gains his object by increasing the number of the knights in each century.*

Mox Lucumōni nōmen Tarquinius Priscus datum
est. Rōmānīs conspicuum eum dīvitiae faciēbant.
Rex, fāmā in rēgiam perlātā, Tarquinium ad se
vocāvit.

Ibī publicīs prīvātīsque consiliīs bello domīque 325
intererat: tūtor etiam līberīs rēgis testāmentō est
factus.

Regnāvit Ancus annos quattuor et vīginti:
adeptus erat magnam glōriam domi et mīlitiae.

Rēge mortuo, Tarquinius populum hortābātur ut 330
quam prīmum comitia rēgi creando fierent (pueri
enim prope pūberem aetātem erant): tum pueros
vēnātum mīsit. Ferunt Tarquinium, ōrātiōne ha-
bitā, populum rogāvisse ut regnum sibi trāderet.

Dixit non sōlum Tatium sed etiam Numam perě- 335
grīnos fuisse ; se Rōmam cum coniugē suā vēnisse
et Rōmānīs prōfuisse.

Haec eum dīcentem ingenti consensu populus
Rōmānus regnāre iussit.

Bellum prīmum cum Latīnīs gessit et, oppido 340
capto, praedam magnam est adeptus.

Tum circum maximum dēsignāvit, mūro quoque
lapideo urbem circumdare volēbat, cum Sabīnum
bellum intervēnit.

345 Ad centurias equitum, quas Rōmulus conscri-
pserat, Tarquinius alias addere constituit. Quia
Rōmulus id inaugurāto fēcerat, Attus Nāvius, augur
praestantissimus, rēgem hoc facere vetuit, nisi aves
secundae fuissent.

350 Tum rex īrātus 'dīvīne tu', inquit, 'inaugurā
num haec res quam nunc ego in mente habeo, fieri
possit'.

Cum ille inaugurāto dixisset eam rem fieri posse,
rex respondit se id in animo habere eum novāculā
355 cōtem discissūrum esse : eam caperet et faceret,
quod aves fieri posse portenderent.

Ferunt Attum statim cōtem novāculā discidisse.

Constat Tarquinium de equitum centuriīs nihil
mūtāvisse, sed numerum equitum in singulīs cen-
360 turiīs dūplicāvisse.

XVI

*Tarquinius defeats the Sabines by means of his increased
army. He then proceeds to fortify and drain Rome.
The omens portending the future greatness of Servius
Tullius: the rapid rise of his fortunes. The sons of
Ancus plot to overthrow the usurper and their scheme
is successful.*

Hac parte copiārum auctā iterum cum Sabīnīs
Tarquinius manūs conserit, et victōriam magnam

reportat. Montes Sabīni petēbant; maxima pars
ab equitibus in flūmen pulsa est.

Bello Sabīno perfecto, Tarquinius triumphans 365
Rōmam rediit. Pax dēinde facta est.

Inde pācis opera perficere constituit: et mūro
lapideo, cūius exordium operis Sabīno bello turbātum
erat, urbem cingit, et infima urbis loca, cloācīs in
Tiberim ductīs, siccat.
370

Eo tempore in rēgiā prōdigium mīrābile fuit.
Pueri dormientis, cui nōmen fuit Servius Tullius,
caput arsisse ferunt multōrum in conspectu. ⟋

Cum quīdam familiārium aquam ad restinguen-
dum ignem ferret, regīna dīcitur eum vetuisse 375
puerum excitāre, dōnec suā sponte experrectus esset.
Narrant cum somno et flammam abiisse.

Tum abducto in sēcrētum viro Tanaquil 'videsne',
inquit, 'tu puerum hunc? Haec flamma ei fortūnam
magnam portendit. Eum igitur omni cūrā nūtriā- 380
mus'. Inde puer optimīs artibus ērudītus est ut
ingenium magnā fortunā dignum fieret.

Iuvenis ēvāsit vērē indolis rēgiae, et fīliam ei
suam rex despondit.

Duodēquādrāgēsimo fermē anno, ex quo regnāre 385
coeperat Tarquinius, non sōlum rex sed etiam pātres
maximo honōre Servium Tullium habuērunt.

Tum Anci fīlii duo qui aegrē ferēbant, se pulsīs,
tūtōrem regnum habēre, spērābant se a regno
tūtōrem esse expulsūros: ob haec rēgi insidias 390
parāre coeperunt.

Ex pastōribus duo ferōcissimi ad facinus dēlecti
sunt ut in vestibulo rēgiae rixam simulārent: mox
appāritōres rēgii appropinquant. Inde, cum ambo
395 rēgem appellārent, ad rēgem dūcuntur.

Prīmo apud rēgem inter se altercantur: tum
lictor eos in vicem loqui iubet. Ūnus dīcere
incipit. Dum rex in alterum se vertit, alter secūri
eum percussit ; deīnde ambo fūgērunt.

XVII

*By Tanaquil's advice the death of Tarquinius was concealed
from the people until Servius Tullus, whom she reminded
of the omens in his infancy, was firmly seated on the
throne. The sons of Ancus went into exile. Servius
makes a new census of the people chiefly for military
purposes, and enlarges and strengthens Rome.*

400   Tanaquil statim claudi rēgiam iussit, arbitros
ēiēcit. Et vulnus rēgis cūrat et consilia capit.
Servio vocāto paene exsanguem virum ostendit et
ōrat ut mortem soceri ulciscātur.

'Tuum est', inquit, 'Servi, si vir es, regnum.
405 Ērige te et deos duces sequere. Nunc te illa cae-
lestis flamma excitet. Si tua, re subitā, consilia
torpent, at tu mea consilia sequere.'

Deīnde ex superiōre parte aedium per fenestram
populum Tanaquil allocūta est: rēgem sānē secūri
410 percussum esse; ferrum haud altē in corpus

descendisse ; iam ad se rediisse ; bono animo essent ;
interea Servium Tullium res cūrātūrum esse.

Tum Servius prōdit cum lictōribus, atque in sēde
rēgiā sedens alia dēcernit, de aliīs se rēgem con-
sultūrum esse simulat.   415

Itaque, Tarquinio iam mortuo, per aliquot dies
morte cēlātā, Servius suas opes firmāvit. Tandem,
morte rēgis nuntiātā, Servius, praesidio firmo
mūnītus, voluntāte pătrum regnāvit. Anci līberi
in exsilium iērunt.   420

Servius pācis opera suscēpit : censum instituit :
classes centuriasque ex censu descripsit.   Prima
classis, quae erat opulentissima, arma tulit et
hastas gladiosque habuit : huic cūra erat urbis
custōdiendae.   425

Reliquae classes, prout iīs erat pecūnia minor,
habēbant arma et tēla leviōra. Equitum quoque
numerum auxit.

Censu perfecto, imperāvit ut omnes cīves Rō-
mānī, equites peditesque, in campo Martio prīmā 430
luce adessent. Ibī instructum exercitum lustrāvit.
Aderant mīlia octōgintā cīvium.

Urbi addit duos colles : aggere et fossīs et mūro
urbem circumdat ; ita pōmērium prōfert.

XVIII

The crimes of Tullia and Lucius Tarquinius Superbus.
Their conspiracy against Servius Tullius succeeds and
the old king is brutally murdered. Tullia sets the seal
of impiety on the vile deed by driving her chariot
over the corpse of her father as it lay in the road.

435   Erant duo fīlii Prisci Tarquinii rēgis, Lūcius
Tarquinius et Arruns Tarquinius. Hīs duae
Tulliae, rēgis fīliae, nupserant. Tullia minor, quam
Arruns in mātrimōnium duxerat, cum Lūcio con-
silia cēpit ut coniugem suum occīderet et alteri
440 frātri nūberet.

Tum vēro in dies infestior Tulli senectūs, in-
festius coepit regnum esse. Iam mulier nova
scelera parābat : marīto suo persuādēbat ut pātres
circumīret et prensāret, iuvenes dōnīs alliceret.

445   Tandem Lūcius, ut rem perficeret, cum agmine
armātorum in forum venit et in rēgiā sēde pro cūriā
sedens praecōnem iubet pātres ad rēgem Tarquinium
vocāre. Convēnēre extemplo, alii iam ante conscii,
alii arbitrāti Servium iam occīsum esse.

450   Ibī Tarquinius convīcia Tullio facere coepit :
Tullium servum esse, regnum occupasse, instituisse
censum ut omnia onera prīmōribus cīvitātis im-
pōneret.

Huic ōrātiōni Servius cum intervēnisset, a trepido
455 nuntio vocātus, extemplo a vestibulo cūriae magnā

vōce, 'quid hoc', inquit, 'Tarquini, est? Aususne
es, me vīvo, vocāre pătres aut in sēde meā sedēre?'

Tum Tarquinius veritus ne rex populum movēret,
multo et aetāte et vīribus validior, medium Servium
arripuit et e cūriā per gradūs dēiēcit. Fit fuga 460
rēgis appāritōrum et comitum; ipse paene exsan-
guis ab iīs qui a Tarquinio missi sunt interficitur.

Tullia, carpento vecta in forum, virum e cūriā
vocāvit rēgemque prīma appellāvit.

Inde, dum Tullia āvehitur, aurīga pavidus frēnos 465
inhibuit iacentemque Servium trucīdātum dominae
ostendit.

Foedum inhūmānumque trāditur scelus: Scele-
rātum vīcum vocant, quod Tullia per pătris corpus
carpentum ēgisse dīcitur, et ipsa sanguine paterno 470
respersa ad virum rediisse.

Servius Tullius regnāvit annos quattuor et quădrāgintā, et magnam glōriam fāmamque adeptus
est.

XIX

*Lucius Tarquinius, surnamed Superbus, secures himself on
the throne by killing or exiling his enemies, and by
diminishing the power of the patricians. He sent his
son, Sextus, to Gabii and gained possession of the town
by a series of treacherous tricks.*

Inde Lūcius Tarquinius regnāre coepit, cui Su- 475
perbum nōmen facta dedērunt, quia socerum gener
sepultūrā prohibuit, prīmōresque, quos Servi rēbus
fāvisse crēdēbat, interfēcit.

Conscius male occupandi regni exemplum ab
480 se ipso adversus se capi posse, corpus armătīs
circumsaepsit.   Multos in exsilium mīsit, non-
nullos bonīs multāvit.

Domesticīs consiliīs cīvitātem administrāvit ;
bellum, pācem, foedera, societātes per se ipse, cum
485 quibus voluit, iniussu populi ac senātūs fēcit dirē-
mitque.   Semper auctōritātem pătrum dēminuere
cōnābātur.

Mox Gabīnīs bellum inferre constituit.   Prīmo
nēquicquam urbem vi adortus est, postrēmo fraude
490 ac dolo aggressus est.   Nam simulāvit se bellum
posuisse, et simul Sextum, fīlium suum, Gabios
fugere iussit et pătris in se ipsum saevitiam conqueri.

Sextus benignē a Gabīnīs excipitur et consiliīs
Gabīnōrum interest.   Pariter cum mīlitibus perīcula
495 et labōres patitur ; pecūniam tam mūnificē largītur,
ut non pater Tarquinius potentior Rōmae quam
fīlius Gabiīs sit.

Itaque, vīribus collectīs, ex suīs ūnum Rōmam ad
pătrem mittit, qui Superbum rogāret, quid se facere
500 vellet.   Huic nuntio, ut ferunt, Superbus nihil vōce
respondit.   Rex velut dēlīberābundus in hortum
transit, sequente nuntio fīlii : ibī ambulans tacitus,
summa papāverum capita dīcitur baculo dēcussisse.

Nuntius rediit Gabios.   Narrat quae vīderit :
505 rēgem seu īrā seu superbiā nullam vōcem ēmīsisse.
Sextus tamen intellexit quid pater vellet ; deīnde
prīmōres accūsāvit alios apud populum, alios sēcrēto

interfēcit. Multi sponte suā fugērunt, multi in
exsilium missi sunt. Dēnique urbs, orba consilio
auxilioque, rēgi Rōmāno sine proelio trāditur.   510

XX

*Tarquinius now turns his attention to improvements in the
city. Owing to strange portents appearing he sends his
sons and Brutus to Delphi to inquire about their meaning. The young men carry out his orders and then ask
the oracle which of them is to be the heir to the throne.
They receive an ambiguous answer. Brutus outwits the
young Tarquins.*

Gabiīs captīs Tarquinius ad negōtiā urbāna animum vertit: quōrum erat prīmum, ut Iovis templum in monte Tarpēīo monumentum regni sui
nōminisque relinqueret.   Caput hūmānum intēgrā
faciē aperientibus fundāmenta templi dīcitur appā- 515
ruisse. Haec species portendēbat arcem eam imperii
caputque rērum fore. Deīnde cloācam maximam,
receptāculum omnium purgāmentōrum urbis, sub
terrā agendam cūrāvit.

Dum haec agit, appāruit in rēgiā portentum 520
terribile: anguis ex columnā ligneā ēlapsus terrō-
rem fugamque omnium fēcit et rēgis pectus cūrīs
implēvit.

Itaque Tarquinius Delphos ad maximē inclutum
in terrīs ōrāculum duos fīlios mittere statuit, qui 525
responsa ad se referrent. Mox Titus et Arruns
cum Iūnio Brūto profecti sunt. Hic cum prīmōres

cīvitātis ab avunculo interfectos esse audīvisset, ex
industriā stultitiam simulāvit nec Brūti cognōmen
530 abnuit, ne rex se ipsum timēret. Is tum ab Tarquiniīs ductus est Delphos, lūdĭbrium vērius quam
comes.

Cum Delphos vēnissent rogāvērunt ad quem
regnum Rōmānum esset ventūrum. Ex infimo
535 specu vōcem respondisse ferunt: 'imperium summum Rōmae habēbit qui vestrum prīmus, o iuvenes,
osculum mātri dederit.' Tarquinii inter se constituunt sortīri uter mātri osculum daret. Brūtus
tamen arbitrātus terram esse commūnem mātrem
540 omnium mortālium, prōlapsus terrae osculum dedit.

XXI

*During the siege of Ardea the Roman leaders begin to boast
of the industry of their wives: they decide to make
a surprise visit, and Lucretia, the wife of Tarquinius
Collatinus, is adjudged to be the best housewife. Sextus
Tarquinius falls in love with her. She calls on her
husband to avenge the insult and kills herself. The
Roman citizens, infuriated by the pride and license
of the Tarquins, declare them exiles. The king and
his family are banished and consuls are elected.*

Posteā Rōmāni Ardeam oppugnāre statuunt:
spērāvērunt se prīmo impetu urbem captūros.
Tandem obsidiōne Ardeam cingere coacti sunt.
Mox rēgii iuvenes ōtium convīviīs cōmissātiōnibus-
545 que inter se terēbant.

Dum pōtant apud Sextum Tarquinium, de
uxōribus loqui coeperunt: suam quisque laudat.
Collātīnus affirmāvit Lūcrētiam uxōrem suam cēte-
rīs praestāre.. 'Conscendāmus', inquit, 'equos, ut
nostrārum ingénia praesentes invisāmus'.   550
Incaluerant vīno; 'conscendāmus equos', omnes
iterant. Celerrimē equīs vehuntur. Lūcrētiam
inter ancillas lānam ducentem inveniunt, rēgiās
nurūs convīvio tempus terentes. Omnes ūno consensu Lūcrētiam laudant: ipsa virum Tarquinios- 555
que benignē excēpit. Deīnde ab nocturno lūdo in
castra redeunt.

Post paucos dies Sextus Tarquinius, inscio Collā-
tīno, cum comite ūno domum Collātīni venit.
Exceptus benignē Lūcrētiam rogat ut marītum suum 560
dēserat: Lūcrētia abnuit. Sextus ōrat et miscet
precibus minas.

Sexto profecto, Lūcrētia nuntium ad pātrem
virumque mittit; celeriter cum Brūto veniunt.
Hos certiōres facit de minīs et scelere Sexti, tum 565
rogat ut dexteras sibi dent et Sextum pūniant.
Hīs dictīs, cultro, quem sub veste habēbat, cor percussit et moribunda cecidit. Sīc Lūcrētia mortua
est.

Brūtus cultrum ex vulnere Lūcrētiae extraxit et, 570
'vos, dii', inquit, 'testes facio me Lūcium Tarquinium Superbum cum coniuge, cum līberīs Rōmā
expulsūrum esse, nec illos nec alium regnāre Rōmae
passūrum'. Statim omnes eadem iūrant.

575 Corpus Lūcrētiae, domo ēlātum, in forum portant,
excitantque homines maesto spectāculo. Ferocissimus quisque dīcit rēges expellendos esse. Inde
Collātiā profecti, duce Brūto, armāti Rōmam per-
vēnērunt.
580 Ubī Rōmam ventum est, urbs plēna erat pavōre
ac tumultu. Ex omnibus locīs urbis in forum curritur. Ibī ōrātio habita est a Brūto de vi et libīdi-
ne Sexti Tarquinii, de caede miserābili Lūcrētiae.
Praetereā addidit superbiam ipsīus rēgis miseriasque
585 et labōres plēbis quae fossas cloācasque exhaurīre
coacta est. Rōmānos, victōres omnium vīcīnārum
urbium, opifices ac lapicīdas pro bellātōribus factos
esse. Narrāvit quōmodo Servius Tullius occīsus
esset, quōmodo fīlia pātris corpus carpento nefando
590 polluisset.
Haec locūtus incenso populo persuāsit ut imperium rēgi ēriperet atque Lūcium Tarquinium
Superbum cum coniuge līberīsque in exsilium
ageret. Ipse, iūniōribus lectīs armātīsque, Ardeam
595 in castra profectus est, ut exercitum parāret adversus rēgem. Inter hunc tumultum Tullia domo
effūgit, omnibus exsēcrantibus invocantibusque
parentum furias.
De rēbus novīs certior factus rex Rōmam con-
600 tendit ad comprimendum tumultum. Sed Tarquinio clausae sunt portae exsiliumque indictum.
Laeta castra accēpērunt urbis līberātōrem. Sextus
Tarquinius profectus Gabios, tamquam in suum

regnum, ab ultōribus caedis et rapīnae interfectus
est.   Lūcius Tarquinius Superbus regnāverat annos 605
quinque et vīgintī.

Regnātum est Rōmae ab conditā urbe ad līberātam
annos ducentos quādrāgintā quattuor.   Inde duo
consules creātī sunt Lūcius Iūnius Brūtus et
Lūcius Tarquinius Collātīnus.   610

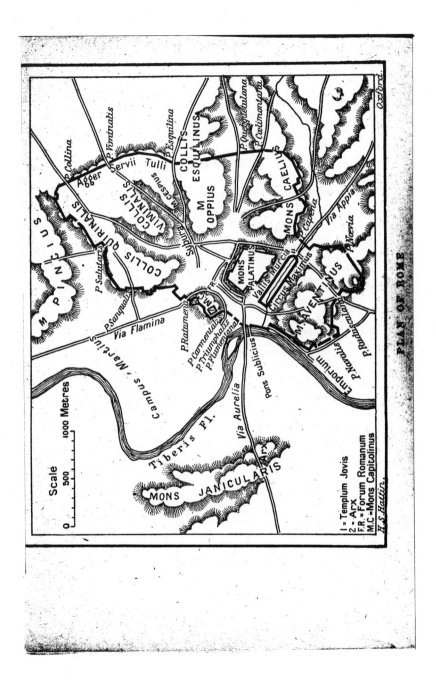

PLAN OF ROME

NOTES

[*L. G.* refers to Allen's *Latin Grammar* (Clarendon Press).]

I

2. decimo anno : abl. of time when. *L. G.* 101, 121, 236. Note that this abl. is not preceded by a preposition, but that the abl. of place usually has *in* before it.

4. Italiam : acc. after *in*, because motion to a place is expressed. *L. G.* 102.

5. Aeneas : nom. because it is in apposition to *dux*, the copulative verb being *est* ; filius is in app. to *Aeneas*. For the meaning of apposition and its three kinds see *L. G.* 98, 99, 100.

8. rex : see on 5.

10. ab Aenea : abl. of agent. *L. G.* 121 (*m*). **proelio** : abl. of manner. *L. G.* 121 (*k*).

11. in matrimonium dedit, 'gave in marriage', as we say ; but note the meaning of *in* with acc., 'into' or 'for the purpose of' marriage.

14. Lavinium appellat : understand *oppidum*, *Lavinium* being acc. in app. to it.

II

16. urbem : acc. in app. to *Lavinium*. **matri** : indirect object after *reliquit*. *L. G.* 116 (*a*).

19. huic oppido : dat. of possessor. *L. G.* 249 and note. We should translate by the genitive here.

20. Mortuo Ascanio : abl. absolute. The word 'absolute' means 'unconnected', and this abl. is so called because it is independent of the rest of the sentence in construction. The phrase consists of a noun or pronoun in the abl. joined to a participle or another noun or an adjective in agreement with it. Notice that what is called a literal translation usually makes poor English. Here, instead of translating 'with Ascanius dead' or even 'Ascanius having died', we should say 'after the death of Ascanius'. See *L. G.* 262 for examples of abl. abs. and the best way of translating them.

22. **factus est** : copulative verb, *rex*, which follows it, being in app. to *Procas*.

24. **Numitori** : indirect object after *legat*. See above, l. 16. **qui** : see *L. G.* 95 (*c*) for the agreement of the relative pronoun with its antecedent. All pronouns agree thus with the noun to which they refer ; the relative is peculiar merely because it is at once a pronoun and a conjunction. **natu** : abl. of respect. *L. G.* 121 (*f*).

29. **Vestalem legit,** ' he appointed Vestal Virgin '. *Vestalem* is in app. to *Ream Silviam*. It was the duty of these Vestals to guard the fire that was always burning in the temple of Vesta, and in later times their office became one of great honour and importance. Amulius made Silvia a Vestal, because he wished to prevent her from marrying and having sons, who might dispute his power. If he had lived two thousand years later, he might have sent her into a convent with the same intention.

III.

30. **Reae Silviae Martique** ... **filii erant** : dat. of possessor.

32. **sacerdotem** : i. e. *Silvia*. **vinciri,** ' to be bound ', i. e. to be put in prison.

33. **iubet** : *iubeo* and *veto* (forbid) take an accus. of the object with an infin. following to explain what the command is. Other verbs of commanding, advising, &c., take *ut* and the subjunctive.

36. **adire** ... **possunt** : for this use of the pres. infin. after such verbs as *wish, begin, be able,* &c., see *L. G.* 273. It is often called the prolative infin. because it carries on (*profert*) the construction and completes the sense of the main verb.

37. **exponere** : again a prolative infinitive, after *constituunt*. **in** ... **stagnis** : abl. of place where, preceded by *in*, as is usual. So in lines 38, 41 just below. *L. G.* 255 note.

44. **lingua** ... **lacte** : ablatives of the instrument.

47. **domum** : note that this acc. has no preposition before it, though it expresses *to* a place. *L. G.* 102, footnote.

IV

50. **Romulus Remusque** : the twin son of Mars and Rea Silvia.

53. **praeda amissa** : abl. absol. **insidiis** ... **vi** : ablatives of manner.

56. eum ... impetum fecisse : an oblique (or indirect) statement. *L. G.* 200 (*a*). The statement is called oblique in this case because it forms the object of a verb, *dicunt*. If it were a *simple* (or direct) statement, i. e. if it stood alone, it would be *is impetum fecit*, 'he made a raid'. When this statement is *oblique*, e. g. if, as here, it forms the object after *dicunt*, ' they say that he made a raid ', the nom. *is* becomes the accus. *eum*, and the indic. *fecit* becomes the infin. *fecisse*. Note that the word 'that' is not translated in the Latin and is often omitted in English ; and that the tense of the infinitive, present, past, or future, follows the tense of the indicative.

57. ad supplicium, 'for punishment '.

58. se educare : an oblique statement, forming the object to *Faustulo spes fuerat*, which is equal in meaning to *Faustulus speraverat*, 'Faustulus had hoped '. Notice that the reflexive pronoun is used because it refers to *Faustulo*, which word is subject in sense, though not in form, to the main verb *speraverat* implied in *spes fuerat*. On the other hand, in l. 56 above we find *eum*, because it does not refer to the subject of the main verb *dicunt*.

60. infantes : subject to the infin. *expositos esse*.

64. in regem, ' on the king '.

<h3 style="text-align:center">V</h3>

70. condere : prolative infin. after *constituunt*.

71. uter ... daret et regnaret, ' which was to give ... and reign ' ; an oblique (or indirect) question, not forming the object of a verb (as is very common) but the subject of *incertum fuit*. *L. G.* 200 (*b*). Oblique questions, as direct questions, are always introduced by some interrogative word (*L. G.* 60), here by *uter*. The verb of the oblique question is in the subjunctive. In this case, however, the verb, even in the direct question, would be in the present subj. *uter ... det et regnet ?* ' which is to give ... and reign ?' For this ' dubitative' use of the subj. in direct questions see *L. G.* 198 (*c*).

73. auguria capere, ' to take auguries ', i. e. to ascertain the divine will, which in this case was to be declared by the appearance of vultures to the rival twins. It was not agreed, however, whether their claims should be decided by the number of birds seen by each, or by the time at which they were seen. Hence the dispute which arose afterwards.

74. prior . . . vidit, 'saw earlier ', i. e. than Romulus, ' was the first to see '.

75. duodecim : understand *vidit*.

79. ut . . . vexaret : a final clause, i. e. a clause that indicates purpose. See *L. G.* 199 (*a*). In English the infin. mood is very often so used, and *ut . . . vexaret* is best translated ' to annoy ', but the infin. must not be used in Latin. Read carefully *L. G.* 300 (note). *ut* is followed, when a purpose is indicated, by the present subjunctive, if the tense of the main verb is *primary*, and by the imperfect subjunctive if the tense of the main verb is *historic.* For primary and historic tenses see *L. G.* 42.

82. pereant : jussive use of the subj. *L. G.* 198 (*e*).

VI

86. duodecim lictores : the name is derived from *ligo* (bind), because these lictors carried an axe tied up in a bundle of rods, or because they tied the hands and legs of those who were to be scourged. They were the regular attendants of the consuls and certain other Roman magistrates, their duty being to disperse the crowd, flog, behead, &c. It was supposed that Romulus took them (*sumpsit*) from the Etruscans, and the number twelve was explained by the fact that there were twelve Etruscan tribes, each of which contributed one lictor to their common king.

89. asylum : this is a Greek word, meaning ' a safe place '.

91. novarum rerum ¢vidi : these three words may be translated ' adventurers ', but understand clearly what the separate words mean.

92. senatores : men chosen for age (*senes*) and wisdom to form the king's council or senate. In later times its number was greatly increased. For many hundred years it constituted the government of the Roman Republic. **patres :** heads of families or, as we might say, of clans, for the family of an aged Roman would include the families of his sons.

94. ut . . . mitteret, ' to send '. *moneo* and other verbs meaning ' to command ', ' to advise ', &c., are followed by *ut* and subj. to express the oblique command. See *L. G.* 200 (*c*), 301, and note on line 33 above.

101. ludos : these were games in honour of Neptune, which Romulus was celebrating as a pretext for inviting the neighbouring peoples to Rome.

104. ut . . . acciperent, 'to accept', following *hortabatur*.
See l. 94, above.

105. Romanis nuberent : the dative follows *nuberent*
because *nubo* is really an *intransitive* verb, meaning 'I veil
myself', and cannot be followed by the acc. So in the next
line resiste' ant, being intransitive, is followed by the dat.
precibus. But in English 'marry' and 'resist' are transitive.

VII

111. praeerat : one of the compounds of *sum*, followed by
the dative. *L. G.* 118 (*a*).

112. Note two cases of apposition in this sentence, *Tar-
peiam* in the acc. in app. to *filiam*, *rex* in the nom. in app.
to *Tatius*.

114. magni ponderis : gen. of quality, with *armillas*. *L. G.*
129 (*d*).

bracchio laevo : notice abl. of place without *in* before
it. This is very uncommon except in a limited number
of expressions. *L. G.* 255 (note). Perhaps, mixed with this
sense, there may be also the 'means' by which the armlets
were carried.

117. dent : jussive use of the subjunctive. See l. 82
above.

121. die postero : abl. of time when. See on l. 2
above.

124. n . . . macularent, 'not to stain'. This clause
follows *orabant* and indicates the *purpose* of the request.
Because purpose is indicated, *ne* is used instead of *ut* . . .
non. *L. G.* 301. If the clause was not final, but consecutive,
i. e. if *result* was expressed, *ut* . . . *non* would be used.

125. enim : this conjunction always follows the first word
in its sentence.

126. uxores : understand *se esse*. It might make the
translation easier if a word meaning 'but' or 'and' was
inserted before *uxores*, but the balance of *filias* and *uxores*
makes this unnecessary. So in English we can say 'the
daughters of the one . . ., the wives of the other'.

VIII

128. Aliquot annos : acc. of duration of time. *L. G.* 101,
235. Tatius : the king of the Sabines. He and Romulus
united their kingdoms and reigned jointly.

130. **ad,** 'for'. **corporis,** 'person'.

132. **ut ... haberet :** a consecutive clause, indicating result. *L. G.* 199 (*b*). **annos :** acc. of duration of time.

139. **luce redeunte :** abl. absolute. Do not suppose that the perf. part. pass. is the only participle used in abl. absolute. It is far the most common.

142. **deo :** abl. of origin. *L. G.* 121 (*b*).

144. **a patribus :** abl. of agent, 121 (*m*). For these *patres* or 'senators' see above, l. 92.

147. **inquit :** this verb is used when the exact words of the speeches are given. It is never followed by the acc. and the infin. It is usually placed after the first or second word of the speech, never before the first word.

149. **his verbis :** abl. of manner. *L. G.* 121 (*k*).

150. **deos velle :** oblique statement, being the object after *nuntia.* **ut ... sit :** clause following *velle* and explaining what the wish of the gods is. After *velle* a prolative infin. or acc. and infin. is common ; an *ut* clause is rare. *L. G.* 301 (exceptions).

152. **ne ullae :** not *ut nullae.* because *purpose* is indicated, not *result.* So we have *ne,* not *ut non,* l. 124, above. **armis :** dat. after the intransitive *resistere.* So l. 106, above.

IX

155. **quis ... adipisceretur :** an oblique question, forming the subject to *incertum erat.* See above, l. 71.

158. **fremere et dicere,** 'began to murmur and to say'. Historic infinitives. *L. G.* 276 and note. This infin. is called *historic* because it is used to relate what happened in the past, just as a past tense of the indic.

161. **visum est,** 'it has seemed good to', 'it has been approved by'. Impersonal pass.

162. **si ... creaveritis,** 'if you elect'. But notice that the tense is fut. perf. to suit the future *comprobabunt.* For this form of conditional sentence see *L. G.* 394 (*b*).

163. **clamare et rogare :** see above, l. 158. **ut ... decerneret :** after *rogare ;* as after *monebant* and *hortabatur,* ll. 94, 104, above.

164. **quis ... regeret :** an oblique question, not as above, ll. 71, 155, a subject, but the object after *decerneret.*

165. **incluta iustitia :** abl. of quality. *L. G.* 121 (*j*).

171. **mores,** 'institutions', such as are mentioned below, l. 176.

173. **persuaderet** : this verb may be followed by a dative of the person persuaded and an accusative of the fact of which he is persuaded. Here the place of a noun in the accus. is taken by the oblique statement *deos hoc velle*, i. e. this statement is the direct object after the verb. hoc : i. e. the giving of justice, &c.

174. **simulat** : as this is a primary tense (see above, l. 79) we might have expected *ut ... persuadeat* in the previous line ; but though *simulat* is present in form, it clearly refers to past time and is in sense historic. These 'historic' presents are common in Latin. *L. G.* 208.

Egeria : one of the Muses, or Camenae, mentioned below, l. 180.

175. **his rebus** : note *rebus*. It is necessary to use *res* for 'thing' or 'things' when the termination of the adj. does not show that it is neuter, even though it may be neuter ; e. g. *haec* alone means 'these things', but you must write *eius rei* and *his rebus*, because *eius* and *his* might be of any gender. Of course *res* is fem. **se docere**, 'instructed him'. The reflexive pronoun does not refer to *deam* the subject of *docere*, but to *rex* the subject of the main verb *simulat*.

177. **ad cursus lunae**, 'according to the courses of the moon', i. e. the revolutions of the moon round the earth. As the mean lunar period, or, in other words, the average time between two new moons, is about 29½ days, a year of twelve months so formed would be about eleven days shorter than the solar year of 365¼ days. Consequently the calendar got out of harmony with the seasons. To remedy this confusion, 'intercalary' or inserted months were added to the year from time to time, but this was done with little knowledge or method, and when Julius Caesar at last reformed the calendar, with the help of a Greek mathematician named Sosigenes, it was found to be 67 days wrong.

182. **annos** : acc. of duration of time. See l. 128, above.

X

185. **ad interregnum res rediit**, 'the government went back to an interregnum', i. e. Rome was again without a king, as it had been without one after the death of Romulus.

188. **regi** : dat. after *dissimilis*. This adj. is followed by a gen. or dat., as is *similis*.

189. Arbitratus : from *arbitror*, a deponent verb. Consequently it has a perfect partic. with an active sense.

194. circumdant : this verb has two meanings, 'to surround' and 'to put round', and the construction varies with the meaning. Here it means 'to surround'. It would be equally good Latin to write *urbi fossam circumdant*, 'they put a trench round the city', *urbi* being dat. of the indirect object.

196. dictatorem : it does not follow that Mettius Fufetius had exactly the same powers as a Roman dictator. He is so called because he was appointed to supreme authority for a time on account of the death of the king during the war.

197. infesto exercitu, 'with his army to attack it'. Phrases formed with *infestus* often cannot be translated quite literally; e. g. l. 214, below, translate *infestis armis . . . concurrunt*, 'they advance in-battle array', not 'with hostile arms'.

200. placet : impersonal use, but like many other impersonals it has an infin. for its subject.

201. rem decernere, 'to decide the issue'. *res* may be translated in a great number of ways. The infin. is subject to *placet*.

202. in duobus exercitibus, 'in each of the two armies'.

204. ferunt, 'they say', i. e. 'it is commonly said'.

206. fratribus hoc placet, 'the brothers agree to this'.

208. ut is populus . . . imperaret : an oblique command, not following a verb of commanding, asking, &c., as is usual, but the phrase *his legibus*, 'on these conditions', which explains what was to be done according to the terms of the treaty, and is therefore equivalent in sense to a verb.

209. vicissent : subjunctive, because it is a subordinate clause belonging to an oblique command. See *L. G.* 200 (c), a very important rule.

XI

213. pro castris : this might seem to refer to one camp only, as *castra* is one of the plur. nouns that are sing. in meaning. The addition of *utrimque* makes the sense clear.

215. consertis manibus, 'when they had joined their (opposing) hands', i. e. when they had begun to fight. In ancient times men mostly fought at very close quarters.

217. cum . . . vidissent : *cum* is followed by the subj. if the sense requires an imperf. or pluperf. tense. *L. G.* 144.

It is important to notice this, because all other conjunctions indicating *time* (temporal conjunctions) are followed ordinarily by the indic.

223. dum ... hortatur, 'was urging', though *hortatur* is present. *dum*, meaning *while*, is followed usually by the pres. indicative, even when the main verb is in a past tense, as *petebat* is here. *L. G.* 147 (a).

226. priusquam ... posset: if the only point is that one thing happened before another, *priusquam* is followed by the indic. If, in addition to this, some *purpose* or *intention* is implied, the subj. is used. In this case Horatius killed the man with the intention of getting rid of him before his companion came up.

230. ferro: abl. of instrument. intactus: understand *erat*. vulnere: abl. of cause.

232. fratrum: gen. after *Manibus* (as a sacrifice); 'to the spirits of my dead brothers'.

233. Romanus Albano: sing., though each of these words implies the whole people. So we talk of 'the Roman', 'the Alban'.

XII

237. trigemina spolia, 'the spoils taken from the three brothers'.

238. desponsa ... fuerat: for the more common *desponsa erat*. uni ex Curiatiis: we might equally well have *uni Curiatiorum*, in which case the gen. would be one of partition. *L. G.* 129 (b).

240. solvit crines, 'lets down her hair', in token of grief.

243. sorori: dat. after *iratus est*.

247. vivi: understand *fratris*, contained in *fratrum*. eat: i. e. to death. For the jussive subj. see l. 82, above.

250. ad regem, 'before the king'.

254. provocatione certatum ad populum est, 'the question was tried before the people on (in consequence of) the appeal'. The king had passed a summary judgement against Horatius, as is shown by the order to the lictor to bind his hands. Horatius, however, says, 'I appeal' to the assembly of the people just mentioned. Then the question was tried, with the result that the people acquitted Horatius. provocatione: abl. of cause. ad populum: after *certatum est*, not *provocatione*, as is proved by the order of the words here and by similar phrases elsewhere.

255. certatum est : lit. ' it was contended ' ; impers. passive. These impersonals are often best translated by a noun and a verb. So l. 275, below, *nuntiatum est*, ' news was brought '.

256. There are two oblique statements in this sentence ; *se iudicare* follows *clamavit*, and *filiam caesam esse* follows *iudicare.*

259. ne . . . faceret : final. See on l. 124, above.

260. admiratione . . . iure : ablatives of cause.

XIII

262. Albam : note the omission of the prep. before the name of a town. *L. G.* 102. qui . . . traducerent : subj. because purpose is indicated. *L. G.* 143, 300. *qui . . . traducebant* would mean ' who were bringing '. This use of the relative and subjunct. is a very common variety for *ut* and the subjunct. and has exactly the same meaning.

264. ad diruendam urbem, ' for (the purpose of) destroying the city '. If the Latin form was the same as the English, we should find *ad diruendum* (gerund) *urbem* (acc. after gerund). But the use of the gerund in Latin is mainly confined to intransitive verbs ; if the verb is transitive, the object (*urbem* here) takes the case of the gerund (the acc.) and the gerundive (instead of the gerund), being an adjective, agrees with the object. It happens that *urbem* is acc. in both forms of the phrase ; and another example may be clearer. In the place of *in liberando urbem*, ' in freeing the city ', we find *in urbe liberanda*, the object *urbem* becoming the abl. after *in* (as the gerund is in the other form of the phrase), and the gerundive (an adj.) agreeing with *urbe.* From the drawing or ' attracting ' the object into the case of the gerund, and the use of the gerundive, the term ' gerundive attraction ' has been given to this construction. The words do not at all explain themselves, and it is worth while to make an effort to understand them.

265. ruinis : abl. of cause.

269. genti : in app. to *Sabinis.*

272. equites : nom. case.

275. nuntiatum est : see on l. 255, above.

276. lapidibus pluvisse, ' that it had rained (with) stones '. *pluvisse* is an oblique statement, subject to *nuntiatum est.* As *pluit* is an impers. verb, this infin. can have no acc. as subject to it.

277. ut . . . facerent : an oblique command following *vocem auditam esse* ; these words are equivalent in sense to a verb of *speaking*.

280. ab armis, 'from war'.

281. militiae . . . domi : locatives. *L. G.* 106.

283. commentarios, 'note books', 'records', of religious observances proper for various occasions. As one of these books was supposed to be like a Roman book, a roll of writing (*volumen*), Tullus is said *volvisse,* to have 'unrolled' or 'studied' it.

285. fecisse : this infin. follows *dicitur,* to which Tullus is the subject. *dicitur* is not ordinarily used as an impers. pass. with an acc. and infin. after it.

XIV

291. filia : abl. of origin. *L. G.* 121 (*b*).

295. hostium, 'of the enemy', i. e. done *by* the enemy. If the sense of the passage allowed, it might also mean 'done *to* the enemy'. In the first case *hostium* is called the subjective genitive, because it indicates the subject, i. e. the persons who commit the outrage. In the second case it is called the objective genitive, because it indicates the object, i. e. the persons on whom the outrage is committed. *L. G.* 128. Subjective genitives are always dependent on nouns ; objective genitives may also be dependent on adjectives. *L. G.* 265 (note 2).

297. postquam . . . pervenit : for the indic. after *postquam* and other temporal conjunctions see on l. 217 above. Note also that *postquam* is followed by the perfect indic., where the pluperf. might seem more natural. *Postquam pervenit* has the same sense as *cum pervenisset.*

298-9. coniecit . . . indicebatur : note the change of tense. *coniecit* is perfect, because it is the single act of a particular herald ; *indicebatur* is imperfect, because it makes a general statement about the ceremony in declaring war.

300. Ancus : the subject to *cepit,* from which it is separated by two ablatives absolute and a deponent participle.

302. urbem, 'the capital'.

304. Ianiculum : a hill on the west of the Tiber and separated by it from the seven hills of Rome. Ancus feared that an enemy might occupy it and make it a stronghold (*arx*) for an attack on the city. **inopia :** abl. of cause.

306. coniungere: this infin. is subject to *placuit*, used impersonally. See l. 200, above.

307. Tarquiniis, 'from Tarquinii'. Note the omission of the preposition. Many names of towns are plural in form.

308. maximi: understand *honoris*, objective genitive. He *expected* high honour; his *ambition* was for the highest.

310. auxit, 'advanced'.

313. forte, 'as it happened', not 'by accident'.

315. capiti: indirect object after *reposuit*.

318. alta sperare, 'to have high hopes', lit. 'to hope high things'. In translating many expressions of this sort we give the sense of a Latin verb by a noun, e. g. *hoc respondit*, 'he made this answer'. **aquilam... venisse:** the acc. and infin. shows that this is an oblique statement, a continuation of Tanaquil's speech. We may say that *dicit* is implied in the preceding *iubet*; it is not necessary or even usual to express it, the construction alone being a sure guide to the sense.

320. secum. *L. G.* 222 (rule).

XV

325. consiliis: dat. after *intererat*, a compound of *sum*. *L. G.* 118 (*a*). **bello:** ablative, with the same sense as the locative *belli*.

326. liberis: dat. of advantage. *L. G.* 117 (*a*). **regis:** depends both on *liberis* and *testamento*.

331. quam primum, 'as soon as possible'. *quam* is very often used to strengthen superl. adjectives or adverbs. **regi creando:** dat. of purpose. *L. G.* 117 (*f*). For the gerundive construction see on l. 264. **pueri... erant:** if any unnecessary time was allowed, one of these sons might become quite grown up and claim to be elected.

333. venatum: to get them out of the way for the present. For the use of this supine see *L. G.* 136.

337. Romanis: dat. after a compound of *sum*.

342. circum maximum: a large oval building between the Palatine and Aventine Hills, for races and games.

345. centurias equitum: three bodies, each consisting of a hundred mounted men, formed by Romulus and Tatius out of the three tribes. Tullus Hostilius had doubled the number of these men (see l. 267 above). Tarquinius doubles it again, thus making 1,200. The bodyguard of Romulus (l. 130) is separate from these.

347. id : i. e. the enrolment of centuries. So *hoc* in the next line.

348. nisi aves secundae fuissent, 'unless the birds had been favourable', i. e. unless he had got good omens from observation of the flight or cry of birds.

349. fuissent : subjunctive, because it is a subordinate clause attached to an oblique command. *L. G.* 201. In this case the oblique command is contained in *facere*, the infin. being used to express it after *iubeo* and *veto.* If the command were direct, we should have the future perfect indic. instead of the pluperf. subj. The augur said to the king, *noli hoc facere, nisi aves secundae fuerint.*

351. num ... posit : subj., as the clause is an oblique question forming an object after *inaugura.* In *oblique* questions *num* does not imply the answer ' no '.

354. id : object after *in animo habere* and explained by the oblique statement *eum ... esse.*

355. caperet et faceret : subjunctives, because they form an oblique command. *L. G.* 200 (c). The actual words of the king were *hanc cape et fac, quod ares fieri posse portendunt.*

358. Tarquinium ... mutavisse : oblique statement forming a subject to the impersonal *constat. L. G.* 200 (a).

XVI

364. flumen : the Anio, which the Sabines must cross to get home.

368. cuius exordium operis, 'a work, the beginning of which'. In English we should put ' work ' in apposition to ' wall '; in Latin it is usual to put it in the relative clause, and consequently in the same case as the relative.

371. eo tempore in regia : notice the two ablatives, of ' time ' without *in*, of ' place ' with *in*.

372. Servius Tullius : his origin and his position in the palace seem to have been uncertain.

373. arsisse : always intransitive. *uro* and *incendo* are transitive.

376. donec ... experrectus esset : pluperf. subjunctive, because the clause is subordinate and attached to the oblique command, contained in *excitare* which follows *vetuisse.* See l. 349, above.

877. et flammam, 'the flame also'.

878. videsne: the interrogative *-ne* is attached to the emphatic word in the sentence, and this word must be placed first. In the absence of any special stress, the verb is the most emphatic word. Hence we have *videsne*. *Tune vides* would mean, 'Is it you that are seeing?'

880. nutriamus. Jussive use.

883. evasit, 'he turned out' or 'he grew up to be'. **indolis:** gen. of quality with *iuvenis*. L. G. 129 (d). *iuvenis* is part of the predicate. L. G. 88 note).

889. tutorem .. habere: oblique statement following *aegre ferebant*. which is equivalent to a verb of *thinking*. L. G. 200 (a) ; 'who were annoyed that'.

390 regi: dat. of disadvantage. L. G. 117 (a).

392. ad, 'for'.

395. ducuntur: historic present. This explains the imperfect *appellarent*, which suits the sense, not the form, of *ducuntur*. See above, l. 174. L. G. 208.

398. securi: abl.

XVII

402. Servio: dat.

403. soceri: Tarquinius. See l. 383, above.

404. vir, 'a true man'.

405. deos duces, 'the gods as guides', or better, 'the guidance of the gods'. *duces* in app. to *deos*.

406. re subita: abl. abs.

407. at, 'at least'.

409. regem, &c.: four oblique statements, showing what Tanaquil said. They are interrupted by the clause *bono animo essent*. Why is the verb in the subjunctive? It cannot be a subordinate clause, as it contains no conjunction. It is therefore a principal clause, i. e. either a question or a command. It cannot be a question because there is no interrogative word. It is therefore an oblique command, representing Tanaquil's actual words, *bono animo este*. This should be carefully noticed, as an oblique command, thus inserted, often proves to be puzzling.

411. ad se rediisse: i. e. had recovered consciousness.

414. aliis: this word might seem to break the rule given above on l. 175, because the termination suits any gender ; but it is clearly neuter, as it balances the preceding *alia*.

421. censum: this valuation of property was made by Servius, so that he might organize the citizens as a body for making laws, electing magistrates, &c., but principally as an army. All the citizens whose property exceeded a certain limit were divided into five classes, the first class consisting of the most wealthy, the second of those next in wealth, and so on to the fifth. Each class was divided into a number of smaller bodies or centuries (which must not be confused with the *centuriae equitum*). Notwithstanding their name, these centuries did not consist of a hundred men, or of any fixed number. The voting was made not by individuals but by centuries; i. e. each century gave a single vote. This arrangement was greatly in favour of the rich, as the first class must have been the smallest in number of members, but contained far more centuries than any other.

423. arma: i. e. defensive armour.

426. prout . . . minor: the expense of the arms was borne by the members of the various classes. The lower classes, therefore, were not required to arm themselves with as costly weapons as the higher.

427. equitum: hitherto there had been 1,200. See on l. 845, above.

431. instructum exercitum lustravit, ' he reviewed his drawn-up army', though accurate, would be very bad English. In such cases it is best to turn the participle into another verb; ' he drew up and reviewed his army '.

432. milia octoginta civium: see *L. G.* 165 (*a*).

433. duos colles: the Quirinal and Viminal on the north of the city.

434. pomerium: this space, on both sides of the wall, marked with boundary stones, was the limit within which the city auspices could be taken. Thus when Servius extended the line of the wall he extended the *pomerium* also.

XVIII.

436. duae Tulliae: the Romans had no special names for women; all the daughters of a family were called by the feminine form of the father's *nomen*, i. e. the name of his clan. Thus the daughter of Marcus Tullius Cicero was called Tullia. If there were several daughters, they were distinguished by *maior, minor, tertia, quarta,* &c.

439. alteri fratri: i. e. Lucius, who was to kill his own wife, the elder Tullia.

441. infestior, 'more insecure'. **senectus**: understand *coepit esse.*

442. regnum, 'royal authority', 'throne'.

444. circumiret et prensaret: he is to make a regular canvass as a candidate might do at a political election.

446. pro curia, 'in the front of the senate house', not 'outside', as we shall soon see.

447. regem: so Tarquin styles himself in the summons.

450. Tullio: dat. of disadvantage.

451. Tullium servum esse: this and the following oblique statements are objects to a verb of 'speaking' implied in *convicia facere.* **occupasse,** 'had usurped'.

452. omnia onera: this is an exaggeration. He had made the rich pay more than the poor.

457. me vivo: pronoun and adjective forming abl. abs.

458. veritus ne ... moveret: the ordinary construction after verbs of fearing. *L. G.* 387.

459. multo: abl. of measure, with *validior. L. G.* 121 (*g*).

465. dum ... avehitur: for the present after *dum*, though the main verb *inhibuit* is past, see on l. 223, above. **frenos**: from *frenum*, one of the 'heterogeneous' nouns. *L. G.* 163 (*c*).

469. vocant: understand some object, e. g. *locum*, to which *Sceleratum vicum* is in apposition. **per patris corpus**: notice the genitive placed, as an adjective might be, between the preposition and the noun that follows it.

XIX

475. Superbum, 'the Cruel'; acc. in apposition to, not in agreement with, *nomen.*

476. socerum gener: these words are put together for the sake of emphasis, but *gener* is unnecessary to the sense. If Servius was the *socer* of Tarquin, it is superfluous to say that Tarquin was *gener.* We give emphasis by saying 'his own father-in-law', just as superfluously.

477. quos Servi rebus favisse credebat: it is plain that *quos ... favisse* is an oblique statement after *credebat*, just as *eos ... favisse* might have been. But when the acc. is the relative pronoun, a difficulty arises in translation. 'Whom he believed to have favoured' may sound literal, but it is not English. In such cases the best way is to put the verb of saying, thinking, &c. (*credebat* here), into a parenthesis. 'Who had, as he believed, favoured the interests of Servius'.

479. conscius, 'knowing', followed by the oblique statement 'that an example ... could be taken'. ab se ipso, 'from himself'.

480. corpus, 'his person'. armatis : there is no *ab* before this ablative, as there would be if it was abl. of agent after a pass. verb. These 'armed men' are *instruments* of which Tarquin disposes.

482. bonis multavit, 'punished in (respect of) their property', i.e. fined.

483. domesticis, 'private', i.e. 'personal', as opposed to a policy formed in concert with senate or people.

492. in, 'against'.

496. ut non ... sit : result is expressed, and therefore *ut non*, not *ne*, is used.

498. ex suis : understand *viris*.

499. mittit : historic present ; hence the imperfect subjunctives which follow. qui ... rogaret : the subj. implies purpose, just as it would if it followed *ut*. *L. G.* 143. See l. 262 above. se : i.e. Sextus, the subject of *mittit*, not the messenger, the subject of *rogaret*.

504. viderit : subj. in oblique question.

509. consilio auxilioque : abl. of separation after *orba*. *L. G.* 121 (*a*).

XX

511. animum, 'attention'.

513. monte Tarpeio : part of the Capitoline hill, above the rock down which criminals were thrown. monumentum, 'as a memorial', in app. to *templum*.

514. integra facie, 'with features perfect ' ; abl. of quality with *caput*.

515. aperientibus : dat. after *apparuisse*, 'to them opening ' or 'digging', the same in sense as *dum aperiunt*, 'while they were digging'.

516. arcem eam ... fore : note the gender of the pronoun *eam*. As is usual, it follows the gender of the predicate (*L. G.* 88 note), 1.e. *arcem* in this case.

517. caput rerum, 'the capital of the world'. cloacam maximam : we have already heard of sewers (l. 369 above) made by Tarquinius Priscus. This great sewer was built to drain the ground between the Palatine and the Tiber, and still exists and serves the purpose of its builder.

519. agendam : this use of the gerundive instead of the infin. after *curo* is peculiar but regular. *L. G.* 281.

525. duos filios, 'two of his sons', for he had more than two.

526. referrent : subj. indicating purpose.

527. Iunio Bruto: he was the son of the king's sister, Tarquinia. The name *Brutus*, or the 'Dullard', was given him on account of his feigned stupidity.

529. Bruti: gen. defining *cognomen*. *L. G.* 129 (*c*).

531. ludibrium, 'a butt', in app. to *is*. **verius:** adv.

534. esset venturum : for the sequence of tenses in the oblique question see *L. G.* 148. Here the actual words of the question would be *ad quem regnum Romanum veniet ?* The periphrastic conjugation (*L. G.* 73) must be used when the fut. indic. is changed into the fut. subj.

536. habebit : as subject understand *is*, the antecedent to *qui*. **vestrum :** from *tu*, gen. of partition. *L. G.* 129 (*b*).

538. uter . . . daret: oblique question. In this case notice that if the question were direct, we should find *uter det ?* 'which is to give ?' (dubitative use, *L. G.* 198 (*c*)), not *uter dat?* 'which is giving?' See above, l. 71.

XXI

542. capturos : understand *esse*.

545. inter se, 'with each other'.

547. suam quisque : notice the order. The cases of *se* and *suus* regularly precede *quisque*.

548. Collatinus: Tarquinius of Collatia, so called because he was governor of that town.

550. praesentes, 'with our own eyes'.

553. regias nurus : i.e. the wives of the *regii iuvenes*, mentioned l. 544, above.

556. ludo, 'adventure'.

562. minas : i.e. he threatened to accuse her of infidelity to her husband.

566. ut dexteras sibi dent : they were to 'give their right hands' as a pledge that they would punish Sextus. Notice that the reflexive *sibi* refers not to the subject of *dent* in the oblique command but to the subject of the main verb, *rogat*.

571. me . . . expulsurum esse, nec . . . passurum : these oblique statements form objects after a verb of 'saying', implied in *vos testes facio*.

573. illos . . . regnare : acc. and infin. is regular after *patior* as after *sino*.

576. ferocissimus quisque, ‘all the most violent’. This use of *quisque* and the superlative is very common ; if it is the subject, the verb is always singular.

580. ventum est, ‘it was come’ (by them) ; i.e. ‘they came’. This use of intransitive verbs impersonally in the passive (*L. G.* 39) is common in Latin. So *curritur* in the next line.

585. plebis : here used generally for the ‘poor people’. fossas : i.e. the smaller drains.

586. Romanos . . . factos esse : this follows some verb of saying that may easily be understood, as Brutus is making a speech.

591. incenso populo : not abl. abs. but dat. after *persuasit* ; ‘he angered the people and persuaded it’.

592. regi : indirect object after *eriperet*. For this dat. of separation, translated by ‘from’, see *L. G.* 117 (*d*).

598. parentum furias, ‘the avenging spirits of parents’, i.e. the spirits that avenge wrong done to parents. *parentum* does not refer specially to Tullia’s *parents*. It is not related that she wronged her mother.

600. Tarquinio, ‘against Tarquin’ ; dat of disadvantage.

601. exsilium . . . indictum, ‘sentence of banishment was proclaimed’.

607. regnatum est : impers. pass., ‘government by kings lasted’. See on l. 255, above. ab condita urbe, ‘from the foundation of the city’. In this and in many similar phrases we translate the Latin participle by a noun.

608. duo consules : they held office for one year only. Thus the royal power was not only divided but limited in time.

VOCABULARY OF PROPER NAMES

Aenē-as, -as, Aeneas, a Trojan hero and ancestor of the kings of Rome.

Alb-a Long-a, -ae . . . -ae, f., a city in Latium, built by Ascanius.

Albān-i, -ōrum, m. plur., the people of Alba.

Albānus, adj., of Alba Longa.

Albān-us Mon-s, -i . . . -tis, m., the hill of Alba.

Amūli-us, -i, king of Alba, brother of Numitor.

Anc-us Marti-us, -i . . . -i, the fourth king of Rome.

Arde-a, -ae, f., a town of Latium, south of Rome.

Arruns, see Tarquinius.

Ascani-us, -i, m., son of Aeneas.

Asi-a, -ae, f., Asia Minor, Asia.

Attus, see Navius.

Aventīn-us Mon-s, -i . . . -tis, m., also Aventīn-um, -i, n., the Aventine, one of the seven hills of Rome.

Brūt-us, -i, Jūnius Brūtus, nephew of Tarquinius Superbus: he drove out the kings and was first consul of Rome.

Caenīnens-es, -ium, plur., the people of Caenina, a town in Latium.

Camēn-a, -ae, f., a muse, an Italian goddess of arts and literature.

Camp-us Marti-us, -i . . . -i, m., the field of Mars, outside the gates of Rome.

Celer-es, -um, m. plur., the knights who formed the body-guard of Romulus.

Cluili-us, -i, a king of Alba Longa.

Collāti-a, -ae, f., a town near Rome.

Collātīnus, adj., of Collātia, a name of Tarquinius Collatinus, nephew of Tarquinius Priscus and husband of Lucretia.

Curiāti-i, -ōrum, m. plur., the three Alban brothers of this name who fought against the Roman Horatii.

Delph-i, -ōrum, m. plur., a town in Greece, the seat of the famous oracle of Apollo.

Ēgeri-a, -ae, one of the Roman muses: the wife and adviser of Numa Pompilius.

Faustul-us, -i, the shepherd who reared Romulus and Remus.

Fufeti-us Metti-us, -i ... -i, a dictator of Alba Longa.

Gabi-i, -ōrum, m. plur., a city of Latium near Rome.

Gabin-i, -ōrum, m. plur., the inhabitants of Gabii.

Graecus, adj., Greek, of Greece.

Horāti-i, -ōrum, m. plur., the three Roman brothers who fought against the Curiatii of Alba Longa.

Horāti-us, -i, Publius Horatius, the father of the three Horatii.

Hostili-us, see Tullus Hostilius.

Iānicul-um, -i, n., the hill on the Tiber, on the river bank opposite to Rome.

Itali-a, -ae, f., Italy.

Iuppiter, Iovis, Jupiter, the father and king of the Roman gods.

Lārenti-a, -ae, wife of Faustulus, who helped to bring up Romulus and Remus.

Latīnus, adj., of Latium, Latin; as subst. the people of Latium.

Latin-us, -i, Latinus, a king of one of the towns of Latium.

Lāvini-a, -ae, daughter of Latinus, married to Aeneas.

Lāvini-um, -i, n., a city in Latium, founded by Aeneas, and called after Lavinia.

Lūcrēti-a, -ae, wife of Tar- quinius Collatinus.

Lucum-o, -ōnis, a citizen of Tarquinii who came to Rome and assumed the name of Lucius Tarquinius Priscus: he became the fifth king of Rome: killed by the sons of Ancus Martius.

Măn-es, -ium, m. plur., the spirits of the dead.

Mar-s, -tis, m., the god of war, Mars.

Martius, Ancus, see Ancus.

Mettius, Fufetius, see Fufetius.

Navius, Att-us Navi-us, -i . . . -i, an augur who opposed Tarquinius Priscus.

Num-a Pompili-us, -ae ... -i, the second king of Rome, renowned for his piety.

Numit-or, -ōris, king of Alba Longa, son of Procas, brother of Amulius.

Pompilius, see Numa.

Priscus, see Lucumo.

Procas, king of Alba Longa, father of Numitor and Amulius.

Procul-us, -i, a Roman senator who reported the deification of Romulus.

Quirīt-es, -ium, m. plur., an old name of the Roman people.

Rē-a Silvi-a, -ae . . . -ae, a Vestal, mother of Romulus and Remus.

Rem-us, -i, Remus, twin-brother of Romulus.

Rōm-a,-ae, f., Rome,founded by Romulus: the future capital of Italy and of the Roman empire.

Rōmānus, adj., Roman. Rōmān-i, -ōrum, m. plur., the Romans.

Rōmul-us, -i, the founder and first king of Rome.

Sabīnus, adj., Sabine, an Italian tribe near Latium. Sabīn-i, -ōrum, m. plur., the Sabines. Sabīn-a, -ae, a Sabine woman.

Scelerāt-us Vīc-us, -i . . . -i, m., the accursed street where Tullia drove over the body of her father.

Servius, see Tullius.

Sextus, see Tarquinius.

Silvia, see Rea.

Silvi-us, -i, king of Alba Longa.

Spuri-us Tarpei-us, -i . . . -i, a Roman in command of the citadel, father of Tarpeia.

Superbus, see Tarquinius.

Tanaqu-il, -īlis, wife of Lucius Tarquinius Priscus.

Tarpei-a, -ae, the treacherous daughter of Spurius Tarpeius; she betrayed Rome to the Sabines.

Tarquini-i, -ōrum, m. plur., locative Tarquiniīs, one of the chief cities of Etruria.

Tarquini-us, -i, the family name of the Tarquins. (1) Lūcius Tarquinius Priscus, see Lucumo. (2) Lūcius Tarquinius Superbus, son of Tarquinius Priscus, the seventh and last king of Rome, finally banished from the city. (3) Arruns Tarquinius the elder was a brother of Tarquinius Superbus, and was murdered by him and Tullia. (4) Arruns Tarquinius the younger and (5) Titus Tarquinius were sons of Tarquinius Superbus: (6) Sextus Tarquinius, son of Tarquinius Superbus, won Gabii treacherously, but was killed later by the Gabines. (7) Tarquinius Collātīnus, nephew of Tarquinius Priscus, see Collatinus.

Tiber-is, -is, m., the Tiber, the river flowing past Rome.

Tit-us Tati-us, -i . . . -i, a Sabine king and joint king with Romulus of the Sabines and Romans.

Troi-a, -ae, f., Troy, the home of Aeneas.

Troiānus, adj., Troiān-i, -ōrum, m. plur., the Trojans.

Tulli-a, -ae, the younger daughter of Servius Tullius, wife of Lucius Tarquinius Superbus: she murdered her first husband Arruns Tarquinius.

Tulli-a, -ae, the elder

daughter of Servius Tullius, married Tarquinius Superbus, but was murdered to enable him to marry her younger sister.

Tulli-us, -i, Servius Tullius, the sixth king of Rome, a great reformer and builder : killed by Tarquinius Superbus.

Tull-us Hostili-us, -i . . . -i, the third king of Rome, a warlike king : killed by a thunderbolt.

Ven-us, -eris, f., goddess of love, mother of Aeneas.

Vestāl-is, -e, adj., belonging to Vesta, the goddess of the hearth : as subst., a Vestal virgin consecrated to the service of the goddess.

Vicus, see Sceleratus.

LATIN-ENGLISH VOCABULARY

ABBREVIATIONS

a, ab, prep. w. abl., *from, by, on the side of.*

abdū-co, -xi, -ctum, 3, *lead away.*

ab-eo, ab-īvi or **-ii, -itum, -īre,** *go away, depart.*

abnu-o, -i, -itum, 3, *refuse.*

ab-ripio, -ripui, -reptum, 3, *seize.*

absol-vo, -vi, -ūtum, 3, *acquit.*

ab-sum, -fui, -esse, *be absent, distant.*

ac, see **atque.**

ac-cēdo, -cessi, -cessum, 3, *advance to, approach.*

ac-cipio, -cēpi, -ceptum, 3, *receive, admit, welcome, hear.*

accūso, 1, *accuse.*

aci-es, -ēi, f., *line of battle, army, battle.*

ad, prep. w. acc., *to, at, near.*

ad-do, -didi, -ditum, 3, *add.*

adeo, adv., *to such a degree, so.*

ad-eo, -īvi or **-ii, -itum, -īre,** *approach.*

·ad-icio, -iēci, -iectum, 3, add. apply.

·ad-ipiscor, -eptus, 3 dep., obtain, gain.

·ad-iuvo, -iūvi, -iūtum, 1, assist, help.

·administro, 1, administer, manage.

·admīrāti-o, -ōnis, f., admiration.

·ad-orior, -ortus, 4 dep., attack.

·ad-sum, -fui, -esse, be present.

·adversus, adv. and prep. w. acc., towards, against.

·advolo, 1, fly to.

·aed-es, -is, f., temple; in pl., house.

·aeg-er, -ra, -rum, adj., sick, ill.

·aegrē, adv., with difficulty; w. fero, pati, feel annoyed at.

·aetas, -ātis, f., lifetime, age.

·affirmo, 1, assert, say.

·ag-er, -ri, m., field, land.

·agg-er, -eris, m., mound.

·aggredior, aggressus, 3 dep., attack.

·agm-en, -inis, n., army, column, band.

·ag-nosco, -nōvi, -nitum, 3, recognize.

·ago, ēgi, actum, 3, act, drive, build; w. praedam, plunder; from driving cattle, the chief sort of booty.

·aio, aiunt, def., say.

·aliquot, indecl. adj., some, considerable number of.

·ali-us, -a, -ud, adj., other, another; alii ... alii, some ... others.

·al-licio, -lexi, -lectum, 3, win over.

·allo-quor, -cūtus, 3 dep., speak to, address.

·al-o, -ui, -tum, 3, keep, support, suckle.

·altē, adv., deeply, deep.

·alter, -a, -um, adj., the one or the other of two, another; alter ... alter, the one ... the other.

·altercāti-o, -ōnis, f., dispute.

·altercor, 1 dep., dispute.

·altus, adj., high, deep.

·alve-us, -i, m., hollow vessel, basket.

·ambo, num. adj., both.

·ambulo, 1, walk.

·amīc-us, -i, m., friend.

·ā-mitto, -mīsi, -missum, 3, lose.

·ample-ctor, -xus, 3 dep., embrace.

·ancill-a, -ae, f., handmaid, slave.

·angu-is, -is, m. and f., snake.

·anim-us, -i, m., mind, courage, attention.

·ann-us, -i, m., year.

·ante, adv. and prep. w. acc., before.

·aper-io, -ui, -tum, 4, open, open up, disclose.

·appāreo, 2, appear, be plain.

·appārit-or, -ōris, m., attendant (of officials).

·appello, 1, address, name, call, appeal to.

·appropinquo, 1, approach.

·apud, prep. w. acc., in the presence of, at the house of.

·aqu-a, -ae, f., water.

·aquil-a, -ae, f., eagle.

·arbit-er, -ri, m., witness (not in the legal sense).

arbitror, 1 dep., think.

ar-deo, -si, -sum, 2, *burn.*

arm-a,-ōrum, n. pl.. *arms (especially of defensive armour* .

armill-a, -ae, f., *bracelet, armlet.*

armo, 1, *arm* ; armāti, *armed men.*

ar-ripio, -ripui, -reptum, 3, *seize, snatch up.*

ar-s, -tis, f., *art, skill* ; plur., *accomplishments.*

ar-x, -cis, f., *citadel (especially of the Capitol in Rome), fortress.*

asȳl-um, -i, n., *sanctuary, place of refuge.*

at, conj., *but, yet, at least.*

atque, or ac, *and.*

ǎtr-ox, -ōcis, adj., *fierce, dreadful, horrible.*

auctōrit-as,-ātis, f., *influence, authority.*

·au-deo, -sus, 2 semi-dep., *dare.*

audio, 4, *hear, listen to.*

aufero, abstuli, ablātum, auferre, *take, carry away.*

au-geo, -xi, -ctum, 2, *increase, strengthen.*

aug-ur, -uris, m., *augur, soothsayer, interpreter of omens and signs.*

auguri-um, -i, n., *augury.*

aureus, adj., *golden.*

aurīg-a, -ae, m. and f., *charioteer.*

·aur-um, -i, n., *gold.*

aut, conj., *or* ; aut . . . aut, *either . . . or.*

auxili-um, -i, n., *aid, help, assistance.*

āve-ho, -xi, -ctum, 3, *carry away* ; āvehor, *drive away.*

avidus, adj., *desirous, eager.*

av-is, -is, f., *bird, omen.*

avuncul-us, -i, m. *mother's brother, uncle.*

bacul-um, -i, n., *stick. staff.*

bellāt-or, -ōris, m.. *warrior.*

bellicōsus, adj., *warlike.*

bell-um, -i, n., *war.*

benignē, adv., *kindly, in a kindly spirit.*

bonus, adj., *good* ; n. plur., *goods, property.*

bracchi-um, -i, n., *arm.*

brev-is, -e, adj., *short.*

ca-do, cecǐdi, cāsum, 3, *fall.*

caed-es, -is, f., *slaughter, murder.*

caedo, cecǐdi, caesum, 3, *kill, cut down.*

caelest-is, -e, adj., *heavenly.*

cael-um, -i, n., *heaven, sky.*

camp-us, -i, m., *level ground, plain* ; = Campus Martius, *the plain of Mars outside Rome.*

capess-o, -īvi, -ītum, 3, *take in hand, take to.*

capio, cēpi, captum, 3, *take, take up, take prisoner, adopt (a plan), choose.*

cap-ut, -itis, n., *head, capital.*

carpent-um, -i, n., *a two-wheeled carriage.*

castr-a, -ōrum, n. pl., *camp.*

caus-a, -ae, f., *cause, case.*

celeriter, adv., *quickly* ; superl., celerrimē.

cēlo, 1, *hide, conceal.*

cens-us,-ūs, m.,*census, rating, rateable property.*

centum, num. adj., *hundred.*

centuri-a, -ae, f., *body of*

hundred, century; one of the divisions of the classis in the Servian constitution.

certām-en, -inis, n., *contest, struggle, engagement.*

certo, 1, *strive, contend.*

certus, adj., *certain, sure;* certiōrem (-es) facio, *inform;* certior fieri, *be informed.*

[ceterus,-a,-um], adj., *more common in the plur., the rest, remaining.*

cin-go, -xi, -ctum, 3, *surround.*

circā, adv. and prep. w. acc., *round, around.*

circum-do, -dedi, -datum, 1, *surround, put round.*

circum-eo, -īvi or -ii, -itum, -īre, *go round, canvass.*

circumsaep-io, -si, -tum, 4, *fence round, guard.*

circ-us, -i, m., *circus (especially of Circus Maximus).*

cīv-is, -is, m. and f., *citizen.*

cīvit-as, -ātis, f., *state.*

clāmo, 1, *shout.*

clang-or, -ōris, m., *noise, scream (of an eagle).*

class-is, -is, f., *fleet, a class or division in the Servian constitution.*

clau-do, -si, -sum, 3, *shut.*

cloāc-a,-ae, f., *sewer, drain (especially of the Cloaca Maxima in Rome).*

coep-i, -tus, def., *began, have begun.*

cognōm-en, -inis, n., *family name, nickname.*

cōgo, coēgi, coactum, 3, *compel, force.*

colligo, 1, *bind.*

col-ligo, -lēgi, -lectum, 3, *gather together, collect.*

coll-is, -is, m., *hill.*

collo-quor, -cūtus, 3 dep., *talk with, converse.*

colo, colui, cultum, 3, *worship, cultivate, celebrate.*

column-a, -ae, f., *pillar.*

com-es, -itis, m. and f., *companion.*

cōmissāti-o, -ōnis, f., *revel, carousal.*

comiti-a, -ōrum, n. plur., *assembly of citizens at Rome for electing magistrates and passing laws.*

commentāri-us, -i, m., *notebook, memoranda:* generally in plur.

commūn-is, -e, adj., *in common, shared by all.*

com-primo, -pressi, -pressum, 3, *crush, quell.*

comprobo, 1, *confirm, approve, ratify.*

con-cido, -cidi, no sup., 3, *fall in battle.*

concili-um, -i, n., *council, meeting.*

conclāmo, 1, *shout together, shout loudly.*

concur-ro, -ri, -sum, 3, *run, rush together, charge.*

con-do, -didi, -ditum, 3, *found, compose, hide.*

con-gredior,-gressus,3 dep., *come together, meet.*

con-icio, -iēci, -iectum, 3, *fling, hurl.*

coniun-go, -xi, -ctum, 3, *unite, join together.*

coniu-x, -gis, m. and f., *wife, husband.*

cōnor, 1 dep., *try, attempt.*

con-queror, -questus, 3 dep.,
complain of.

consoen-do, -di, -sum, 3,
mount.

conscius, adj., *conscious, privy
to ; as subst., conspirators.*

conscrī-bo, -psi, -ptum, 3,
enrol.

consens-us, -ūs, m., *unani-
mity, consent.*

conse-quor, -cūtus, 3 dep.,
overtake.

conser-o, -ui, -tum, 3 w.
manūs or proelium, *join
battle.*

con-sīdo, -sēdi, -sessum, 3,
sit down, settle.

consili-um, -i, n., *advice, de-
sign, plan, statesmanship.*

conspect-us, -ūs, m., *sight,
gaze.*

conspicuus, adj., *conspicuous.*

constat, 1, impersonal, *it is
agreed.*

cons-ul, -ulis, m., *consul; one
of the two chief magistrates at
Rome, elected yearly.*

consul-o, -ui, -tum, 3, *con-
sult, ask the advice of.*

conten-do, -di, -tum, 3, *strive,
march.*

contrā, adv. and prep. w. acc.,
*against, opposite, towards, on
the contrary.*

con-venio, -vēni, -ventum,
4, *come together, meet, agree.*

convīci-um, -i, n., *abuse, re-
proach.*

convīvi-um, -i, n., *banquet,
feast.*

convoco, 1, *summon.*

co-orior, -ortus, 4 dep., *rise.*

cōpi-a, -ae, f., *plenty;* in plur.,
forces.

corp-us, -oris, n., *body.*

cor-rumpo, -rūpi, -ruptum,
3, *corrupt, bribe.*

cō-s, -tis, f., *whetstone.*

crē-do, -didi, -ditum, 3, with
dat., *believe.*

creo, 1, *elect, appoint.*

cresco, crēvi, crētum, 3, *grow,
increase.*

crīn-is, -is, m., *hair;* usually
in plur.

cult-er, -ri, m., *knife.*

cult-us, -ūs, m., *cultivation,
mode of life.*

cum, conj., *when, since.*

cum, prep. w. abl., *with.*

cupīd-o, -inis, f., *ambition,
desire.*

cūr-a, -ae, f., *care, anxiety.*

cūri-a, -ae, f., *senate-house.*

cūro, 1, *manage, administer,
attend to (of wounds).*

curro, cucurri, cursum, 3,
run, move quickly.

curs-us, -ūs, m., *course, revolution.*

custodi-a, -ae, f., *guard.*

custōdio, 4, *guard, watch, defend.*

de, prep. w. abl., *down from,
concerning.*

de-a, -ae, f., *goddess.*

decem, num. adj., *ten.*

dē-cerno, -crēvi, -crētum, 3,
decide, make a decree.

decimus, num. adj., *tenth.*

declāro, 1, *declare.*

dē-cutio, -cussi, -cussum, 3,
strike off.

dē-do, -didi, -ditum, 3, *give
up, surrender.*

dēfen-do, -di, -sum, 3, *defend,
protect.*

dē-icio, -iēci, -iectum, 8, *throw down.*

dēin, see dēinde.

dēinde -or dēin, adv., *then, after that, next.*

dēlā-bor, -psus, 3 dep., *glide down.*

dēliberābundus, adj., *in deep thought.*

dē-ligo, -lēgi, -lectum, 8, *select, choose.*

dēmin-uo, -ui, -ūtum, 8, *lessen, decrease.*

dēmum, adv., *at last.*

dēnique, adv., *lastly, finally.*

densus, adj., *thick.*

dē-pōno, -posui, -positum, 8, *lay down, lose.*

descendo, -di, -sum, 8, *.descend, penetrate.*

descri-bo, -psi, -ptum, 8, *arrange, draw up.*

dēser-o, -ui, -tum, 8, *abandon, neglect.*

dēsigno, 1, *mark out.*

despon-deo, -di, -sum, 2, *betroth.*

destit-uo, -ui, -ūtum, 8, *leave, desert.*

de-us, -i, m., *god.*

dexter-a, -ae, dextr-a, -ae, f., *right hand.*

dī-co, -xi, -ctum, 8, *say, speak, call.*

dictātor, -ōris, m., *dictator ; a supreme magistrate appointed in Rome at great crises : he superseded all other magistrates.*

di-es, -ēi, m., *day;* in dies, *daily.*

dignus, adj. w. abl., *worthy, worthy of.*

dīmico, 1, *fight.*

dir-imo, -ēmi, -emptum, 8, *break off.*

dīr-uo, -ui, -utum, 8, *demolish, plunder.*

di-scindo, -scidi, -scissum, 8, *cut in two.*

dissimil-is, -e, adj., *unlike, different.*

dissipo, 1, *separate, scatter.*

diu, adv., *for a long time.*

dīv-es, -itis, adj., *rich.*

dīv-ido, -īsi, -īsum, 8, *divide.*

dīvīn-us, -i, m., *diviner, soothsayer.*

dīviti-ae, -ārum, f. plur., *riches.*

do, dedi, datum, 1, *give, grant.*

doc-eo, -ui, -tum, 2, *teach, prove.*

dol-us, -i, m., *deceit, stratagem.*

domesticus, adj., *belonging to home, domestic, private.*

domin-a, -ae, f., *mistress, lady.*

domin-us, -i, m., *master, lord.*

dom-us, -ūs, f., *house, home ;* domum, *to home ;* domi, locative, *at home.*

dōnec, conj., *until.*

dōn-um, -i, n., *gift.*

ducenti, num. adj., *two hundred.*

dū-co, -xi, -ctum, *lead, carry, build, spin;* w. in mātrimōnium, *marry.*

dum, conj., *while.*

du-o, -ae, -o, num. adj., *two.*

duodecim, num. adj., *twelve.*

duodēquādrāgesimus, num. adj., *thirty-eighth.*

dūplico, 1, *double.*

dux, ducis, m. and f., *leader, general.*

e, ex, prep. w. abl., *from, out
of, in accordance with* ; ex
industriā, *on purpose.*

ēduco, 1, *bring up, rear.*

efforo, extuli, ēlātum, effer-
re, *carry out, lift.*

ef-fugio, -fūgi, -fugitum, 3,
flee away, escape.

ef-fundo, -fūdi, -fūsum, 3,
pour out, flood, scatter.

ego, mei, pers. pron., *I.*

ē-gredior, -gressus, 3 dep.,
go out, disembark.

ē-icio, -iēci, -iectum, 3, *turn
out.*

ēlā-bor, -psus, 3 dep., *slip
out, escape.*

ē-mitto, -mīsi, -missum, 3,
utter, send out.

enim, conj., *for.*

eo, īvi or ii, itum, īre, *go.*

equ-es, -itis, m., *horseman,
knight,* in plur., *cavalry.*

equitāt-us, -ūs, m., *cavalry.*

equ-us, -i, m., *horse.*

ē-rigo, -rexi, -rectum, 3,
rouse.

ēripio, -ripui, -reptum, 3,
take away.

ērudio, 4, *educate.*

et, conj., *and, also, even* ; et
. . . et, *both . . . and.*

etiam, adv., *also, even.*

ēvā-do, -si, -sum, 3, *turn out
(to be).*

ex, see e.

ex-cipio, -cēpi, -ceptum, 3,
welcome.

excito, 1, *arouse.*

exclāmo, 1, *cry out.*

exempl-um, -i, n., *example.*

exercit-us, -ūs, m., *army.*

exhau-rio, -si, -stum, 4,
drain out, clean.

exordi-um, -i, n., *beginning.*

expello, -puli, -pulsum, 3,
drive out.

exper-giscor, -rectus, 3 dep.,
awake.

ex-pōno, -posui, -positum,
3, *expose.*

exsangu-is, -e, adj., *bloodless,
lifeless.*

exsēcror, 1 dep., *curse, exe-
crate.*

exsili-um, -i, n., *exile, banishment.*

exsulto, 1, *triumph.*

extemplo, adv., *at once.*

extraho, -traxi, -tractum, 3,
draw out.

faci-es, -ēi, f., *appearance.*

facin-us, -oris, n., *deed,
crime.*

facio, fēci, factum, 3, *do,
make, appoint, offer (sacrifices)* ; w. certiōrem, see
under certus.

fact-um, -i, n., *deed.*

fām-a, -ae, f., *fame, reputation.*

familiār-is, -e, adj., *belonging to the family* ; as subst.,
servant, friend.

fas, indecl. n., *right, divine
law.*

fastus, adj., *a day on which it
is allowed to speak* (i. e. *in
law-courts*), *work days* (opp. to
nefastus, when no business
was allowed).

fāt-um, -i, n., *fate, destiny.*

faustus, adj., *prosperous, for-
tunate.*

faveo, fāvi, fautum, 2, w.
dat., *be favourable.*

fēmin-a, -ae, f., *woman.*
fenestr-a, -ae, f., *window.*
fermē, adv., *nearly, about.*
fero, tuli, lātum, ferre, *carry, bear, say* ; w. aegrē, *see under* aegrē.
fer-ox, -ōcis, adj., *bold, fierce, warlike* ; ferōcior, ferōcissimus.
ferr-um, -i, n., *iron, sword.*
fessus, adj., *tired, weary.*
fīli-a, -ae, f., *daughter.*
fīli-us, -i, m., *son.*
fīn-is, -is, m., *boundary* ; plur., *territory.*
fīo, fieri, factus, *be done, be made, be held, take place.*
firmo, 1, *strengthen.*
firmus, adj., *strong.*
flamm-a, -ae, f., *flame.*
flēbiliter, adv., *tearfully.*
fluito, 1, *float.*
flūm-en, -inis, n., *stream, river.*
foedus, adj., *horrible, detestable.*
foed-us, -eris, n., *treaty.*
fon-s, -tis, m., *spring.*
fore, fut. inf. sum.
forte, adv., *by chance.*
fortūn-a, -ae, f., *fortune.*
for-um, -i, n., *forum, market-place.*
foss-a, -ae, f., *ditch, trench.*
frag-or, -ōris, m., *crash.*
frāt-er, -ris, m., *brother.*
frau-s, -dis, f., *deceit.*
frem-o, -ui, -itum, 3, *murmur.*
frēn-um, -i, n., *bit, rein* ; plur., frēna and frēni.
frustrā, adv., *in vain.*
fug-a, -ae, f., *flight.*
fugio, fūgi, fugitum, 3, *flee.*
fugo, 1, *put to flight.*

fulm-en, -inis, n., *lightning, thunderbolt.*
fundāment-um, -i, n., *foundation.*
furi-a, -ae, f., *avenging spirit. a fury.*
futūrus, fut. partic. of sum.

gaudi-um, -i, n., *joy.*
geminus, adj., *twin.*
gen-er, -eri, m., *son-in-law.*
gen-s, -tis, f., *people, race, tribe.*
gero, gessi, gestum, 3, *carry, carry on, wage (war), wear.*
gladi-us, -i, m., *sword.*
glōri-a, -ae, f., *glory, renown.*
grad-us, -ūs, m., *step.*

habeo, 2, *have, hold, deliver (a speech).*
hast-a, -ae, f., *spear.*
haud, adv., *not.*
hēr-es, -ēdis, m. and f., *heir.*
hic, haec, hoc, demonstr. pron., *this.*
hic, adv., *here.*
hinc, adv., *hence, from here.*
hodiē, adv., *to-day.*
hom-o, -inis, m. and f., *human being, man.*
hon-os, -ōris, m., *honour.*
hortor, 1 dep., *encourage, exhort.*
hort-us, -i, m., *garden.*
host-is, -is, m. and f., *foe, enemy.*
hūc, adv., *hither.*
hūmānus, adj., *of man, human.*

iaceo, 2, *lie.*
iam, adv., *by this time, already.*

ibĭ, adv., *there.*

ĭc-o, -i, -tum, 3, *strike* ; w. foedus, *make a treaty (from the striking of the victims killed in the sacrifice which solemnized the making of the treaty).*

īdem, eadem, idem, pron., *the same.*

igitur, conj., *then, therefore.*

ign-is, -is, m., *fire.*

ill-e, -a, -ud, demonstrat. pron., *that, he, she, it.*

illūc, adv., *thither.*

imperi-um, -i, n., *command, power.*

impero, 1, w. dat., *hold authority, command, order.*

impet-us, -ūs, m., *attack, charge, raid.*

im-pleo, -plēvi, -plētum, 2, *fill, fulfil.*

implicitus, adj., *attacked, infected.*

im-pōno, -posui, -positum, 3, *impose.*

in, prep. w. acc., *in, into, to* ; in dies, *daily* ; w. abl., *in, upon, on.*

inaugurāto, adv., *after taking auspices.*

inauguro, *take auspices, consecrate, divine.*

incal-esco, -ui, no sup., 3, *grow warm.*

incen-do, -di, -sum, 3, *set on fire, anger.*

incertus, adj., *uncertain.*

in-cido, -cidi, -cāsum, 3, *fall on.*

in-cipio, -cēpi, -ceptum, 3, *begin.*

inclutus, adj., *famous.*

incursi-o, -ōnis, f., *invasion.*

inde, adv., *then, after that, thence.*

indī-co, -xi, -ctum, 3, *declare, proclaim.*

indol-es, -is, f., *natural qualities, character.*

industri-a, -ae, f., *diligence* ; ex industriā, *on purpose.*

infan-s, -tis, m. and f., *infant.*

infero, intuli, illātum, inferre, *bring on* ; w. bellum, *make war on.*

infestus, adj., *hostile, dangerous, insecure.*

infimus, adj. superl., *lowest, end of, bottom of.*

ingeni-um, -i, n., *nature, disposition.*

ingen-s, -tis, adj., *enormous, vast.*

in-gredior, -gressus, 3 dep., *go in, enter.*

inhibeo, 2, *check.*

inhūmānus, adj., *inhuman, brutal.*

in-icio, -iēci, -iectum, 3, *cast on, into.*

initi-um, -i, n., *beginning.*

iniūri-a, -ae, f., *outrage.*

iniussu, adv., *without orders.*

inopi-a, -ae, f., *want, poverty.*

in-quam, -quit, def., *say.*

inscius, adj., *ignorant.*

insidi-ae, -ārum, f. plur., *ambush, plot.*

instit-uo, -ui, -ūtum, 3, *appoint, institute.*

instru-o, -xi, -ctum, 3, *set in order, array, draw up.*

intactus, adj., *untouched, fresh.*

integ-er, -ra, -rum, adj., *intact, fresh, unwounded.*

intel-lego, -lexi, -lectum,
3, *understand*.

inter, prep. w. acc., *among,
between*.

intereā, adv., *in the meantime*.

inter-ficio, -fēci, -fectum, 3,
kill.

interim, adv., *in the meantime*.

interregn-um, -i, n., *interregnum, interval between two
reigns*.

inter-rex, -rēgis, m., *inter-
rex, a magistrate acting as
regent between two reigns*.

inter-sum, -fui, -esse, *be
among, take part in*.

inter-venio, -vēni, -ventum,
w. dat., *interfere, interrupt*.

intrā, prep. w. acc., *within*.

intro, 1, *enter*.

in-venio, -vēni, -ventum, 4,
find.

invī-so, -si, -sum, 3, *go to
see*.

invoco, 1, *call on*.

ips-e, -a, -um, pron., *self*.

īr-a, -ae, f., *anger*.

ir-ascor, -ātus, 3 dep., *be
angry*; īrātus, *angry*.

is, ea, id, pron., *that, he, she, it*.

ita, adv., *so, thus*.

itaque, conj., *and so, therefore*.

it-er, -ineris, n., *journey,
march*.

itero, 1, *repeat*.

iterum, adv., *a second time,
again*.

iubeo, iussi, iussum, 2, *bid,
order*.

iūdico, 1, *judge, find guilty of*.

iūnior, comparat. of iuvenis,
younger.

iūro, 1, *swear*.

iūs, iūris, n., *law, justice,
rights*; iūre, *rightly*; iūra,
code of laws; in ius rapere,
carry off to judgement.

iussu, adv., *by the order of*.

iustiti-a, -ae, f., *justice*.

iuven-is, -e, adj., *young*; as
subst., *young man*.

lab-or, -ōris, m., *labour, toil*.

lac, lactis, n., *milk*.

laetus, adj., *glad, rejoicing*.

laevus, adj., *on the left, left*.

lamb-o, -i, -itum, 3, *lick*.

lān-a, -ae, f., *wool*.

lapicīd-a, -ae, m., *stone-cutter,
mason*.

lapideus, adj., *of stone*.

lap-is, -idis, m., *stone*.

largior, 4 dep., *bestow la-
vishly*.

lătr-o, -ōnis, m., *robber*.

laudo, 1, *praise*.

lēgāti-o, -ōnis, f., *embassy*.

lēgāt-us, -i, m., *ambassador*.

legi-o, -ōnis, f., *legion, pro-
perly 6,000 men in 10 cohorts,
60 centuries*.

lego, lēgi, lectum, 3, *select,
choose*.

lēgo, 1, *bequeath, leave (by will),
commission*.

lev-is, -e, adj., *light*.

lex, lēgis, f., *law, proposal,
term, condition*.

liber, adj., *free*.

līberāt-or, -ōris, m., *deliverer,
rescuer*.

līber-i, -ōrum, m. plur.,
*children (only in relation to
parents)*.

lībero, 1, *set free*.

lĭbĭd-o, -ĭnis, f., *eager desire, lust.*

lict-or, -ōris, m., *lictor, attendant on a magistrate.*

ligneus, adj., *wooden, of wood.*

lingu-a, -ae, f., *tongue, language.*

loc-us, -i, m., *place, position*; plur., loci or loca.

longus, adj., *long.*

lo-quor, -cūtus, 3 dep., *speak, say.*

lūc-us, -i, m., *grove (sacred to a god).*

lūdĭbri-um, -i, n., *sport, mockery, joke.*

lūd-us, -i, m., *game*; plur., *public games.*

lū-geo, -xi, -ctum, 2, *mourn.*

lūm-en, -inis, n., *light.*

lūn-a, -ae, f., *moon.*

lup-a, -ae, f., *she-wolf.*

lustro, 1, *purify, review.*

lux, lūcis, f., *light*; primā lūce, *at daybreak.*

maculo, 1, *stain, pollute.*

maestus, adj., *sad, gloomy.*

magis, comp. adv., *more, rather.*

magist-er, -ri, m., *master.*

magnus, adj., *great, large, (of voice) loud.*

male, adv., *evilly, by evil means.*

mando, 1, *entrust, commission.*

man-us, -ūs, f., *hand, band, troop*; w. conserere, *join battle.*

marīt-us, -i, m., *husband.*

māt-er, -ris, f., *mother.*

mātrimōni-um, -i, n., *marriage*; in mātrimōnium dūcere, *to marry.*

maximē, adv. superl., *most, chiefly.*

maximus, adj. superl., *greatest*; w. nātu, *eldest.*

medius, adj., *middle, in the middle*; medium Servium arripit, *seizes Servius by the waist*; as subst., medi-um, -i, n., *centre, middle.*

mem-or, -oris, adj., *mindful, remembering.*

men-s, -tis, f., *mind.*

mens-is, -is, m., *month.*

meus, possess. pron., *my, mine.*

mĭgro, 1, *emigrate.*

mīl-es, -itis, m., *soldier, soldiery.*

mīlitār-is, -e, adj., *military*; res mīlitāris, *warfare.*

mīliti-a, -ae, f., *military service*; mīlitiae, locative, *at war.*

mille, adj. indecl., *thousand*; plur., mīlia, mīlium, subst.

min-a, -ae, f., *threat.*

min-or, -us, comp. of parvus, *less, younger.*

mīrābil-is, -e, adj., *wonderful.*

miserābil-is, -e, adj., *pitiable.*

miseri-a, -ae, f., *misery.*

mitto, mīsi, missum, 3, *send, throw.*

mod-us, -i, m., *manner.*

moeni-a, -um, n. plur., *walls, fortifications.*

moneo, 2, *advise, warn.*

mon-s, -tis, m., *mountain, hill.*

monument-um, -i, n., *monument, record.*

morb-us, -i, m., *illness, disease.*

mor-ior, -tuus, -i, dep., *die.*

mor-s, -tis, f., *death.*

mortāl-is, -e, adj., *mortal*; as subst., *man.*

mō-s, -ris, m., *custom, manner*; in plur., *morals, manners.*

moveo, mōvi, mōtum, 2, *move, agitate.*

mox, adv., *soon, presently.*

muli-er, -eris, f., *woman.*

multitūd-o, -inis, f., *multitude, numbers.*

multo, 1, *punish*; w. bonīs, *fine.*

multus, adj., *much, many,* abl. multo, *by much, far.*

mūnificē, adv., *bountifully.*

mūnio, 4, *fortify, strengthen, build.*

mūr-us, -i, m., *wall.*

mūto, 1, *change.,*

nam, namque, conj., *for.*

narro, 1, *relate.*

nascor, nātus, 3 dep., *be born*; nātus, as subst., *son*; nātu maximus, *eldest.*

nē, conj., *lest, that . . . not, not . . . to*; prohibitive, *do not . . . .*

nĕ, interrog. particle.

nē . . . quidem, adv., *not even.*

neo, neque, conj., *and not, nor*; nec . . . nec, neque . . . neque, *neither . . . nor.*

necto, nexui or nexi, nexum, 3, *weave, plan.*

nefandus, adj., *impious.*

nefastus, adj., *unholy, unlucky*; see fastus.

nego, 1, *deny, refuse.*

negōti-um, -i, *task, work.*

nepō-s, -tis, m., *grandson.*

neque, see nec.

nēquicquam, adv., *to no purpose, in vain.*

nihil, indecl. subst., *nothing.*

nimb-us, -i, m., *cloud.*

nisi, conj., *unless, if not.*

noctu, *at night.*

nocturnus, adj., *at night.*

nōm-en, -inis, n., *name, reputation.*

non, adv., *not.*

nonnullus, adj., *some, several*; usually in plur.

nos, see ego.

nost-er, -ra, -rum, possess. pron., *our.*

novācul-a, -ae, f., *razor.*

novus, adj., *new, fresh, strange*; res novae, *change, revolution.*

no-x, -ctis, f., *night.*

nū-bo, -psī, -ptum, 3, with dat., *marry (of a woman marrying a man).*

nullus, adj., *no, none.*

num, interrog. particle (expecting answer 'no'), *whether.*

numer-us, -i, m., *number.*

nunc, adv., *now, at the present time.*

nuntio, 1, *announce, report.*

nunti-us, -i, m., *messenger.*

nur-us, -ūs, f., *daughter-in-law.*

nusquam, adv., *nowhere.*

nūtrio, 4, *nurse, rear.*

ob, prep. w. acc., *on account of, for.*

oblī-viscor, -tus, 3 dep., *be forgetful, careless*; usually w. genit.

obsidi-o, -ōnis, f., *blockade.*

occī-do, -di, -sum, 3, *kill.*

occultus, adj., *hidden, secret.*

occupo, 1, *seize.*
octōgintā, num. adj., *eighty.*
omn-is, -e, adj., *all, every.*
on-us, -eris, n., *load, burden.*
opif-ex, -icis, m., *workman.*
oppid-um, -i, n., *town.*
op-primo,-pressi,-pressum, 3, *overwhelm, crush.*
oppugno, 1, *assault, attack.*
op-s, -is, f., *strength, aid;* plur., *resources, wealth, power.*
opulentus, adj., *rich.*
op-us, -eris, n., *work.*
ōrācul-um, -i, n., *oracle.*
ōrāti-o, -ōnis, f., *speech;* w. habēre, *to deliver a speech.*
orb-is, -is, m., *circle;* orbis terrārum, *world.*
orbus, adj., *deprived of, childless.*
ord-o, -inis, m., *rank.*
or-ior, -tus, 4 dep., *spring, arise, be born.*
ōro, 1, *pray, beg.*
oscul-um, -i, n., *kiss.*
osten-do, -di, -tum or -sum, 3, *show, declare.*
ostento, 1, *display.*
ōti-um, -i, n., *peace, rest.*

paene, adv., *almost.*
papāv-er, -eris, n., *poppy.*
par, adj., *equal, a match for.*
paren-s, -tis, m. and f., *parent.*
pariter, adv., *equally.*
paro, 1, *prepare, make ready.*
par-s, -tis, f., *part.*
past-or, -ōris, m., *shepherd.*
pat-er, -ris, *father, senator, patrician.*
paternus, adj., *of a father.*
patior, passus, 3 dep., *suffer, allow.*

pătri-a, -ae, f., *fatherland, country.*
paucus, adj., *small, few.*
paulo, adv., *a little.*
pavidus, adj., *frightened.*
pav-or, -ōris, m., *fear.*
pax, pācis, f., *peace;* cum bonā pace, *with complete goodwill.*
pect-us, -oris, n., *breast.*
pecūni-a, -ae, f., *money.*
pec-us, -oris, n., *cattle.*
ped-es, -itis, m., *foot-soldier, infantry.*
pello, pepuli, pulsum, 3, *expel, drive back.*
per, prep.w.acc., *through, over.*
per-cutio, -cussi, -cussum, *strike.*
perĕgrīnus, adj., *foreign;* as subst., *foreigner.*
per-eo, -īvi or -ii, -itum, -īre, *perish.*
per-fero,-tuli, -lātum, -ferre, *bring.*
per-ficio, -fēci, -fectum, 3, *finish.*
per-fugio, -fūgi, -fugitum, 3, *escape, flee.*
perīcul-um, -i, n., *danger.*
perītus, adj., *skilled in;* w. genit.
permultus, adj., *very much, very many.*
persuā-deo, -si, -sum, 2, with dat., *persuade.*
perturbo, 1, *agitate, alarm.*
per-venio, -vēni, -ventum, 4, *arrive, reach.*
pestilenti-a, -ae, f., *pestilence, plague.*
pet-o, -īvi or -ii, -ītum, 3, *beg, seek, make for, attack.*
pīle-us, -i, m., *felt cap.*

placeo, 2, w. dat., *please.*

placet, placuit, 2, impersonal w. dat., *it seems good, it is decided.*

plebs, plēbis or plēbēi, f., *plebs, commons.*

plēnus, adj., *full.*

pluit, plūvit or pluit, 3, impersonal, *it rains.*

plūrimum, adv. superl., *most.*

poll-uo, -ui, -ūtum, 3, *pollute, defile.*

pōmēri-um, -i, n., *pomerium, space inside and outside the walls left free from buildings.*

pond-us, -eris, n., *weight.*

pōno, posui, positum, *lay aside, break off (war), pitch (a camp).*

pon-s, -tis, m., *bridge.*

popul-us, -i, m., *people.*

port-a, -ae, f., *gate.*

porten-do, -di, -tum, 3, *portend.*

porto, 1, *carry.*

possum, potui, posse, *be able, can.*

post, adv. and prep. w. acc., *after, behind, afterwards.*

posteā, adv., *afterwards.*

postquam, conj., *after that, when.*

postrēmo, adv. superl., *lastly.*

poten-s, -tis, adj., *powerful.*

pōto, 1, *drink.*

praec-o, -ōnis, m., *herald.*

praed-a, -ae, f., *booty, plunder.*

prae-mitto, -mīsi, -missum, 3, *send in advance.*

praesen-s, -tis, adj., *present.*

praesidi-um, -i, n., *guard.*

praestantissimus, adj. superl., *famous.*

prae-sto, -stiti, -stātum, 1, *excel*; w. dat.

prae-sum, -fui, -esse, *be in command of*; w. dat.

praetereā, adv., *besides.*

precor, 1 dep., *pray.*

prenso, 1, *interview, canvass.*

prec-es, -um, f. plur., *prayers.*

prīmōr-es, -um, m. plur., *chieftains, nobles.*

prīmus, adj., *first*; prīmum, *in the first place*; prīmo, *at first.*

pri-or, -us, adj. comp., *former*; prius, adv., *before.*

priusquam, conj., *before that.*

prīvātus, adj., *private, individual.*

pro, prep. w. abl., *in front of, before, instead of.*

prō-cēdo, -cessi, -cessum, 3, *advance.*

procell-a, -ae, f., *storm.*

procul, adv., *far, from afar.*

prōd-eo, -īvi or -ii, -itum, -īri, *come forward.*

prōdigi-um, -i, n., *portent.*

proeli-um, -i, n., *battle.*

prō-fero, -tuli, -lātum, -ferre, *bring forward, extend.*

pro-ficiscor, -fectus, 3 dep., *set out.*

prohibeo, 2, *prevent, forbid.*

proinde, adv., *accordingly.*

prōlā-bor, -psus, 3 dep., *fall forward.*

prope, adv. and prep. w. acc., *near.*

propero, 1, *hasten.*

prōpugnāt-or, -ōris, m., *champion, defender.*

prosum, -fui, prodesse, *be useful, benefit.*

prout, adv., *according as.*

provōcāti-o, -ōnis, f., *appeal.*
prŏvoco, 1, *appeal.*
proximus, adj. superl., *nearest, last.*
pūb-er, -eris, adj., *grown up.*
publicus, adj., *belonging to the people, public.*
puell-a, -ae, f., *girl.*
pu-er, -eri, m., *boy;* in plur., *children, infants.*
pugn-a, -ae, f., *battle.*
pūnio, 4, *punish.*
purgāment-um, -i, n., *refuse, filth.*
puto, 1, *think.*

quădrāgintā, num. adj., *forty.*
quam, conj., *than, as, how;* w. superl., quam celerrime, *as quickly as possible.*
quattuor, num. adj., *four.*
-que, conj. *and;* -que . . . -que, -que . . . et, *both . . . and.*
queror, questus, 3 dep., *complain.*
qui, quae, quod, relat. pron., *who, which, what.*
quicumque, quaecumque, quodcumque, relat. pron., *whoever.*
quīdam, quaedam, quoddam, indef. pron., *a certain person, thing.*
qui-es, -ētis, f., *rest, quiet.*
quinque, num. adj., *five.*
quis, quid, interrog. pron., *who? what?* indef. pron., *any one, anything.*
quisque, quaeque, quidque, quodque, pron., *each;* w. superl., optimus quisque, *all the best men.*
quod, conj., *because, that.*

quōmodo, conj., *how.*
quoque, conj., *also, too.*

rapīna, -ae, f., *robbery, rapine.*
rap-io, -ui, -tum, 3, *seize, carry off, plunder.*
re-cēdo, -cessi, -cessum, 3, *recede.*
recens-eo, -ui, -um, 2, *review.*
receptācul-um, -i, n., *receptacle.*
re-cipio, -cēpi, -ceptum, 3, *receive, recapture;* w. reflexive pronoun, *betake oneself, retire.*
red-eo, -īvi or -ii, -itum, -īre, *return.*
refero, rettuli, relātum, referre, *bring back.*
rēgi-a, -ae, f., *palace.*
rēgius, adj., *royal, of a king.*
regno, 1, *rule.*
regn-um, -i, n., *kingdom, reign.*
rego, rexi, rectum, 3, *rule, govern.*
re-linquo, -līqui, -lictum, 3, *leave.*
reliquus, adj., *remaining.*
repet-o, -īvi or -ii, -ītum, 3, *seek back;* w. rēs, *demand restitution.*
re-pōno, -posui, -positum, 3, *place back.*
reporto, 1, *bring back, win (a victory).*
res, rei, f., *thing, cause, fortunes, government;* res novae, *revolution.*
re-sisto, -stiti, no sup., 3, *resist.*
resper-go, -si, -sum, 3, *sprinkle.*
re-spicio, -spexi, -spectum, 3, *look back.*

respon-deo, -di, -sum, 2,
answer.
respons-um, -i, n., answer.
restin-guo, -xi, -ctum, 3,
extinguish.
rex, rēgis, m., king.
rīpa, -ae, f., bank.
rix-a, -ae, f., quarrel.
rōb-ur, -oris, n., strength.
rogo, 1, ask, propose (a bill).
ruin-a, -ae, f., overthrow, ruin.

sacerd-os, -ōtis, m. and f.,
priest, priestess.
săcrifici-um, -i, n., sacrifice.
săcro, 1, consecrate, make sacred.
săcr-um, -i, n., sacred rite,
sacrifice.
saeviti-a, -ae, f., cruelty.
salūbr-is, -e, adj., healthy,
salutary.
sāne, adv., certainly.
sangu-is, -inis, m., blood.
scelerātus, adj., accursed.
scel-us, -eris, n., crime.
scio, scīvi, scītum, 4, know.
scūt-um, -i, n., oblong shield.
se or sēsē, sui, reflexive
pronoun, himself, herself,
itself, themselves ; sēcum =
cum se.
sēcrēto, adv., secretly.
sēcrētus, adj., secret ; in
sēcrētum, to a private place,
apart.
sēcum, for cum se.
secundus, adj., following ;
hence (1) second, (2) favourable.
secūris, -is, f., axe.
sed, conj., but.
sedeo, sēdi, sessum, 2, sit.
sēd-es, -is, f., seat, throne.
semper, adv., always.

senāt-or, -ōris, m., senator.
senāt-us, -ūs, m., senate.
senect-ūs, -ūtis, f., old age.
sen-esco, -ui, no sup., 3, grow
old, decay.
sen-ex, -is, m., old man.
septem, num. adj., seven.
sepultūr-a, -ae, f., burial.
se-quor, -cūtus, 3 dep., follow.
serv-us, -i, m., slave.
sēsē, redupl. form of se.
seu, see sīve.
sex, num. adj., six.
si, conj., if.
sīc, adv., so, thus, in this way.
sicco, 1, dry, drain.
siccus, adj., dry.
sign-um, -i, n., sign, signal,
standard.
simulo, 1, pretend.
sine, prep. w. abl., without.
singuli, num. adj., several, one
each.
sinist-er, -ra, -rum, adj., left,
on the left.
sitio, 4, be thirsty.
sīve, or seu, conj., or if ; sīve
. . . sīve, seu . . . seu,
whether . . . or.
soc-er, -eri, m., father-in-law.
societ-as, -ātis, f., alliance.
sōlum, adv., only ; non sōlum
. . . sed etiam, not only . . .
but also.
sōlus, adj., alone.
sol-vo, -vi, -ūtum, 3, loosen.
somn-us, -i, m., sleep.
sor-or, -ōris, f., sister.
sor-s, -tis, f., lot.
sortior, 4 dep., draw lots,
arrange by drawing lots.
speci-es, -ēi, appearance.
spectācul-um, -i, n., spectacle,
sight.

spec-us, -ūs, all genders,
cave.
spēlunc-a, -ae, f., cave.
spēro, 1, hope, expect.
spes, spei, f., hope, expectation.
spolio, 1, plunder, spoil.
spoli-um, -i, n., spoil.
spons-us, -i, m., betrothed,
lover.
sponte, adv., of one's own ac-
cord ; often as subst. w.
suā.
stagn-um, -i, n., pool, stand-
ing water.
statim, adv., at once, immediately.
stat-uo, -ui, -ūtum, 3, decide,
determine, assign.
stirp-s, -is, f., family, off-
spring.
stringo, strinxi, strictum, 3,
draw (a sword).
stultiti-a, -ae, f., folly.
sub, prep. w. acc., under ; w.
abl., under, at the foot of.
subito, adv., suddenly.
subitus, adj., sudden.
sublīm-is, -e, adj., on high,
exalted.
sub-venio, -vēni, -ventum,
4, with dat., help.
sum, fui, esse, to be ; fore,
futurus esse, fut. infin.
summus, adj. superl., highest,
topmost, supreme ; summus
mons, top of the mountain.
sūmo, sumpsi, sumptum, 3,
take.
super, adv. and prep. w. acc.
and abl., above, upon.
superbi-a, -ae, f., pride.
superbus,adj., proud, haughty.
superi-or, -us, comp. adj.,
higher, superior.

super-sum, -fui, -esse, sur-
vive.
supplici-um, -i, n., punishment.
sus-cipio, -cēpi, -ceptum, 3,
undertake.
suus, reflexive possess. pron.,
his, her, its, their own ; sui,
his men, his friends.

tacitus, adj., silent.
tam, adv., so.
tamen, adv., yet, nevertheless.
tamquam, conj., as, as if.
tandem, adv., at length, at last.
tantus, adj., so great.
tēl-um, -i, n., weapon.
tempest-as, -ātis, f., storm.
templ-um, -i, n., temple.
temp-us, -oris, n., time, season.
tero, trīvi, trītum, waste,
spend.
terr-a, -ae, f., land ; terrae,
the world.
terribil-is, -e, adj., terrible.
terr-or, -ōris, m., terror,
fright.
tertius, num. adj., third.
testāment-um, -i, n., will.
test-is, -is, m. and f., witness.
timeo, 2, fear.
tonĭtr-us, -ūs, m., tonĭtru-
um, -i, n., thunder.
torpeo, 2, be torpid, paralysed.
tōtus, adj., whole.
trā-do, -didi, -ditum, 3, hand
over, hand down, record.
trādū-co, -xi, -ctum, 3, lead
across, transfer.
traho, traxi, tractum, 3,
draw, drag.
tranquillus, adj., calm.
trans-eo, -īvi or -ii, -itum,
-īre, cross.

transil-io, -ui, no sup., 4, *leap over.*

trecenti, num. adj., *three hundred.*

trepidus,adj., *alarmed, excited.*

tres, tria, num. adj., *three.*

trĭgeminus, adj., *three at a birth, triple.*

trĭgintā, num. adj., *thirty.*

triumpho, 1, *celebrate a triumph.*

trucīdo, 1, *kill.*

tu, tui, pers. pron., *thou.*

tum, adv., *then.*

tumult-us, -ŭs, m., *uproar.*

turb-a, -ae, f., *crowd.*

turbo, 1, *throw into confusion, interrupt.*

turm-a; -ae, f., *squadron, of about thirty troopers.*

tūt-or, -ōris, m., *guardian.*

tūtus, adj., *safe.*

tuus, possess. pron., *thy, thine.*

ubĭ, adv., *where, when.*

ul-ciscor, -tus, 3 dep., *take revenge, avenge.*

ullus, adj., *any.*

ult-or, -ōris, m., *avenger.*

umer-us, -i, m., *shoulder.*

ūnus, adj., *one, alone.*

urbănus, adj., *of, belonging to the city.*

urb-s, -is, f., *city.*

ut, conj. and adv., *in order that, so that; when, as, how.*

ut-er, -ra, -rum, pron., *which of two ?*

ŭtrimque, adv., *on both sides.*

ux-or, -ōris, f., *wife.*

vacuus, adj., *empty, clear.*

vāgīt-us, -ŭs, m., *crying of children.*

valeo, 2, *be strong.*

validus, adj., *strong.*

veho, vexi, vectum, 3, *carry.*

velut, adv., *as if, even as.*

venio, vēni, ventum, 4, *come.*

vēnor, 1 dep., *hunt, chase.*

verb-um, -i, n., *word.*

vērē, adv., *truly;* comp. vērius.

vere-or, -itus, 2 dep., *fear.*

vēro, adv., *surely.*

ver-to, -ti, -sum, 3, *turn, devote.*

vērus, adj., *true.*

vestibul-um, -i, n., *porch, vestibule.*

vest-is, -is, f., *clothes, garment.*

vet-o, -ui, -itum, 1, *forbid.*

vexo, 1, *annoy, vex.*

vic-em, -is,f., *turn;* in vicem, *in turn.*

vicīnus, adj., *neighbouring.*

victōrĭ-a, -ae, f., *victory.*

vict-or, -ōris, subst. and adj., *conqueror, victorious.*

vīc-us, -i, m., *street.*

video, vīdi, visum, 2, *see, perceive;* videor, *seem good, seem.*

vīgintī, num. adj., *twenty.*

vin-cio, -xi, -ctum, 4, *bind.*

vinco, vīci, victum, 3, *defeat, conquer.*

vīn-um, -i, n., *wine.*

vi-r, -ri, m., *man, husband.*

virg-o, -inis, f., *virgin, maiden.*

virtūs, -ūtis, f., *virtue, courage.*

vis, vim, vi, f., *force, violence;* vīres, *strength.*

vī-vo, -xi, -ctum, 3, *live.*

vivus, adj., *alive, living.*

vix, adv., *scarcely.*
voco, 1, *call, summon.*
volito, 1, *fly.*
volo, volui, velle, *wish, want,*
   be willing.
volunt-as, -ātis, *will, wish,*
   goodwill.

vol-vo, -vi, -ūtum, 3, *roll,*
   open (a book), read.
vox, vōcis, f., *voice* ; plur.,
   words.
vulnero, 1, *wound.*
vuln-us, -eris, n., *wound.*
vult-ur, -uris, m., *vulture.*

ENGLISH EXERCISES

As these exercises are closely connected with the divisions of the Latin text of the same number, continual reference should be made to the corresponding piece of Latin, as similar constructions will be frequently found in both, and some assistance may be gained by comparing the two. The sections in the rules at the head of the exercises refer to Allen's *Latin Grammar*. The rules must in all cases be learnt thoroughly preparatory to attempting the exercises. Words linked by hyphens are to be translated by a single Latin word. (The exercises are divided into classes *A*, *B*; *A* being easy, *B* slightly harder.)

I

RULES. The Three Concords, § 95. (1) The finite verb agrees with its nominative in number and person. (2) The adjective agrees with its substantive in gender, number, and case. (3) The relative qui, quae, quod agrees with its antecedent in gender, number, and person; but in case belongs to its own clause, §§ 222-229. §§ 96, 97. The copulative verbs take the same case after them as before them. § 98. Nouns in apposition must be in the same case. § 99.

A. 1. Troy was a great city.

2. The Trojans inhabited Troy.

3. The Greeks, a brave race, hated the Trojans.

4. The Greeks captured Troy and slew many Trojans.

5. The rest-of the Trojans deserted the city.

B. 1. Aeneas, who was the son of-Venus, led these Trojans.

2. The Trojans, a small band, sought-for Italy.

3. There they fought with Latinus, the king of that land.

4. Aeneas defeated the enemy, who inhabited the country.

5. The Trojans made peace and founded the town Lavinium.

II

RULES. §§ 120, 255 (note). Place where is usually expressed by the preposition in with the ablative. If the place is a town or small island the locative case is used, § 104. § 103. Place whence is expressed by a, ab, or ex, except in the case of the names of towns or small islands, when the preposition is omitted. § 102. Place whither is expressed by ad or in with the accus., unless the place is a town or small island, when the preposition is omitted. § 60. In questions -ne (attached to the first word) asks a question. num expects the answer 'no', nonne, the answer 'yes'.

A. 1. The Trojans lived at Lavinium.

2. At-first Aeneas reigned in the city.

3. After his death Ascanius ruled the Trojans.

4. He decided to go-away from-Lavinium.

5. He marched with many-men to the Alban mount.

B. 1. Did not the Trojans come from-Troy to-Lavinium?

2. Did Aeneas sail from Asia to Italy?

3. Why did Ascanius wish to set-out from-Lavinium?

4. Was he unhappy at-Lavinium? Did the Trojans hate the king?

5. He preferred to give the city Lavinium to his-mother: he founded a new city and reigned at-Alba Longa.

III

RULES. *L. G.* § 273. After verbs *to wish, begin, be able, resolve,* &c., the infin. is added to complete the sense: this

is the complementary or prolative infin.   § 101. Duration
of time (time how long) is put in the accus.   Point of time
(time when) is put in the ablative.

A. 1. Amulius, who was a cruel king, began to reign.

2. He resolved to kill the children of Rea.

3. He decided to throw them into the river.

4. For-many days the Tiber was-overflowing its banks.

5. And-so at-this time no-one was-able to approach the
Tiber.

B. 1. For-a-short time the children lay near the banks.

2. Next day a wolf came to the river from the hills.

3. For-many days the wolf fed the two children.

4. But at-last Faustulus, who was a shepherd, found
Romulus and Remus.

5. He carried the boys home and resolved to bring-up
the two children.

IV

RULES.   § 120 (*c*). The instrument with which a thing is
done is put in the ablat.   § 121 (*m*). The agent by whom a
thing is done is expressed by *a*, *ab* with ablat.   The manner
in which a thing is done is put in the ablat.   The cause of
a thing being done is put in the ablat.   § 16 (*n*).   *With* is
translated by *cum* with the abl. if the noun denotes a living
thing, otherwise the abl. alone is used.

A. 1. The boys, Romulus and Remus, were brought up
by Faustulus, the shepherd.

2. They lived for-many years with the shepherd and
his (*eius*) wife.

3. The young men were captured by robbers : and
Remus was dragged to the king :

4. But Romulus defended himself (*se*) with-great
bravery and escaped.

5. Faustulus and Larentia were terrified at-this news (*res*).

B. 1. By-the-advice of Faustulus Romulus set-out to Numitor.

2. Next day a plan was prepared by the friends of Numitor.

3. They resolved to kill king Amulius by-a-crafty plot.

4. With-great boldness Romulus came with his friends to the palace.

5. They killed Amulius and gave the throne to Numitor, the king's brother.

V

RULES. § 291. When *him, her, it, them ; his, hers, its, theirs* refer to the subject of the sentence, **se, suus** must be used. When *him, her, it, them* do not refer to the subject of the sentence, use **is, ille.** When *his, hers, its, theirs* do not refer to the subject of the sentence, use **eius, illius, eorum, illorum.** **Ipse** meaning '-self' is a demonstrative adj. and agrees with the noun. **Se** meaning 'self' is a reflexive pronoun.

A. 1. For-a-short time Romulus and Remus remained in Alba Longa.

2. Soon they resolved to found a new city.

3. Romulus wished to give his-own name to-the-city.

4. His brother Remus was-unwilling to allow this.

5. Owing-to-this quarrel their friends were alarmed.

B. 1. Remus leaped-over the walls and annoyed his brother.

2. His friends were not able to appease him.

3. Romulus killed his brother with-his-own hand.

4. Romulus called the city Rome by-his-own name.

5. Many of (*ex*) his friends blamed him and called him impious.

VI

RULES. *L. G.* § 116. The dative is used to translate 'to' (except when it means motion), and § 117, 'for' (except when it stands for phrases such as 'on account of', 'on behalf of'). § 198 (*e*). Use the subjunctive to express wishes. § 378. Use the subjunctive with ne to express negative commands or requests in the first and third persons. With second person use noli, nolite with infin.

A. 1. Romulus, the new king, gave laws to-the-Romans.
2. Also he fortified his town with-high walls.
3. Rome was a refuge for-all-men, slaves and free.
4. Romulus said : ' Let all-men remain safe in-Rome '
5. ' Let them not fear their enemies in my city '.

B. 1. Do not blame Romulus for these words.
2. Let-us-understand the plan of the king.
3. He wished to strengthen his throne and to fill his town with-men.
4. He therefore opened a refuge for-all-men who wished to come to-Rome.
5. Let us admire his love of-his-country : nevertheless do not imitate his example.

VII

RULES. *L. G.* §§ 113, 199 (*a*). When 'that', 'to' mean 'in order that', 'in order to', translate by ut with the (§ 146) subjunctive. Ne is used to translate 'not to', 'lest', 'in order that . . . not'. This signifies a purpose. § 199 (*b*). When 'that' means 'so that', translate by ut with the subjunctive, but use (§ 146) ut . . . non to render 'so that . . . not'. This signifies a result or consequence. Learn very carefully § 148, the sequence of tenses : primary tenses must follow primary and historic must follow historic, but, as regards consequence, note the exception, *L. G.* 206 (*b*).

A. 1. Romulus urged women also to come to-Rome.

2. At last the Romans formed a plan to capture women.

3. The Sabines were so angry that they marched against Romulus.

4. In-a-short time they were defeated by the Romans.

5. They sent ambassadors to their friends to ask-for help.

B. 1. Besides the Sabines bribed Tarpeia to admit them (*se*) into the citadel.

2. Tarpeia said: ' Let the Sabines give me what they carry on-their left arms '.

3. She was crushed by their heavy shields and died.

4. The Romans told this story lest others should imitate her example.

5. The women beg both Sabines and Romans not to stain themselves (*se*) with-blood.

VIII

Rules. *L. G.* §§ 112, 211. The acc. and infin. is used after verbs of *saying, perceiving, knowing, thinking,* and similar verbs. The subject of the dependent clause is put in the accus., and the verb of the dependent clause is put in the infin., the verb of the main clause remains the same. ' He says that the army has come.'—Dicit (' he says ', main verb) exercitum (' that the army ', subject of dependent clause in accus.) venisse (' has come ', the verb of the dependent clause in infin.). The verbs retain the same tense in the infin. as they had in the indic. The word ' that ' is often omitted in English.

A. 1. They say that for-many years there were two kings at Rome.

2. We know that Romulus reigned after the death of Tatius.

3. They related that Romulus was born of-a-goddess.

4. And-so many believed that the gods received him into heaven.

5. But many said this: 'Do not believe an empty story: Romulus was killed by his enemies.'

B. 1. Next day a senator announced that Romulus had returned to the earth.

2. Romulus said that Rome would be the capital of the world.

3. And so he urged all Romans to practise warfare lest they should fail.

4. They relate that many Romans believed the words of the senator.

5. Do you believe that this story is true ?

IX

Rules. *L. G.* § 381. After verbs of *hoping, promising, threatening*, the future infin. is always used, and the subject of the dependent clause must be expressed. 'He hopes to come', i.e. 'he hopes that he will come', sperat se venturum esse. § 211. 'I deny' and 'I say that . . . not' are both translated by nego. Never use dico . . . non.

A. 1. At-first many Romans said that Romulus was not dead.

2. The people said that their masters were not kind.

3. Some hoped to have one master instead of a hundred.

4. The senators promised to create a new king.

5. In-a-short time Numa was created king by the Roman people.

B. 1. Numa hoped to give laws to his country, which was already strong.

2. He persuaded the Romans to believe that he discoursed with a goddess.

3. And he promised to help his people by-means-of her wise advice.

4. Some Romans said that they did not believe these words.

5. Numa reigned for many years in-Rome. All Romans knew that the king helped the city to attain power.

X

RULES. *L. G.* § 291. In simple sentences *se* refers to the subject of its own clause. In indirect statement (or accus. and infin.) if the subject of the dependent is the same as that of the main clause *se* must be used (the same rule applies to *suus*), otherwise *eum, eos* (for the possessive *eius, eorum*) must be used to translate *him, them,* &c. ' He replied that he had not given the book to them, but they to him.' **Ille respondit non se iis sed eos sibi librum dedisse.**

A. 1. He said that he would kill his enemy with his-own hand.

2. He threatened to destroy their town with-a-large army.

3. He hoped to pitch his camp near their citadel.

4. They said that their-men would not defeat his troops.

5. Did they not say that they would return next winter and stay at-home ?

B. 1. The two generals asked their champions to fight for their armies.

2. They hoped thus to decide the battle without bloodshed.

3. The two armies hoped that their champions would return home victors.

4. Did they form their plan wisely to avoid much bloodshed?

5. News was brought (it was reported) to Rome that he had won the victory.

XI

Rules. *L. G.* § 802 and § 817. Deponent and semi-deponent verbs have perfect participles with an active meaning, locutus, 'having spoken '='when he had spoken'. These agree as adj. with their subst. Transitive verbs have perfect participles with a passive meaning, amatus, 'having been loved', agreeing with their subst. as an adj., see especially § 817. Wherever it is possible in sentences in which a Latin participle is to be used make the participle agree with the subject or object as required. (1) 'The Romans having defeated the Gauls killed them,' i.e. 'the Romans killed the (having been) defeated Gauls', Romani victos Gallos occiderunt. (2) 'The Gauls were defeated and fled,' i.e. 'the (having been) defeated Gauls fled', Galli victi fugerunt.

A. 1. The two armies having-met-together pitched their camps.

2. The champions having-been-prepared charged.

3. The Romans carried-away their wounded soldiers.

4. Two Romans having-died were buried by their friends.

5. Three Albans having-been-wounded were not able to run quickly.

B. 1. And so the Roman decided to flee and separate the three Albans.

2. Then having-returned to the fight he was able to kill his separated foes.

3. Thus the enemy having-been-destroyed were buried.

4. The generals led-away their defeated soldiers into camp.

5. The Romans carried home their wounded champion.

XII

Rules. *L. G.* § 302. When the verb is intransitive and not deponent, *cum* with the subjunctive (pluperf. if the principal verb is in an historic tense, perf. if the principal verb is in a primary tense) is used to express a perf. part. 'Having returned he said this', *cum rediisset, haec dixit.* The same construction *may* be used when the verb is transitive. 'Having heard this news, he went away', *cum haec audivisset, abiit.*

A. 1. Having-returned to-Rome Horatius saw his sister.

2. When she had seen the spoils she wept.

3. Horatius having-heard her cries was angry with his sister:

4. And when he had drawn his sword he slew her.

5. Having-seen this the Romans begged the king to punish Horatius.

B. 1. The king said : 'Lictor, bind Horatius with-fetters.'

2. But Horatius having-heard this appealed to the citizens.

3. Horatius' father, an old man, having-approached the king, begged him not to kill his son.

4. Having-embraced his son he displayed the spoils captured by Horatius.

5. Having-seen the spoils and heard these words the people resolved to acquit Horatius.

XIII

Rules. *L. G.* § 123. When the participle cannot be brought into agreement with either subject or object to the verb, use the ablative absolute construction, which is formed by a noun in the ablative with the participle in agreement. 'The horse being killed, I will go away', *equo occiso, abibo* : again, if there is no deponent perf. part. this construction is often used instead of cum and the subj. of a transitive verb as explained in XII, 'having heard this news, he went away', his **rebus auditis, abiit.** For different phrases in English which should be translated into abl. abs. in Latin read carefully § 262, and compare § 302.

No more hyphens will be employed unless in exceptional cases.

A. 1. Cavalry being sent to Alba the people were led to Rome.

2. The walls being destroyed the town was abandoned.

3. Having heard this news the Albans were overwhelmed with grief.

4. War being declared the army marched from Rome into the territory of the enemy.

5. Having routed the enemy the Roman cavalry returned home with the plunder.

B. 1. Being informed by the augurs that the gods were angry Tullus decided to offer sacrifices.

2. When the sacrifices had been offered the gods sent a pestilence on the city.

3. Tullus struck by a thunderbolt died.

4. When their king had been killed by the gods the Romans buried him.

5. In a short time the pestilence vanished and the city freed from disease rejoiced.

XIV

Rules. *L. G.* § 317. In this exercise which refers to Exercises XI, XII, XIII (the rules for these should be re-read), the partic. pass., the perf. partic. deponent, the abl. abs., and cum with the subj. must be used at discretion. First see whether there is a deponent partic. which may be used, or try the participial construction; if neither is possible use the abl. abs., and lastly, but only if necessary, use cum.

A. 1. When the king died the Latins declared war against the Romans.

2. Informed of this Ancus led his army hastily collected against the foe.

3. Having prepared everything and having set out he defeated the Latins.

4. After winning this victory he brought many captives home.

5. To these men thus led away he gave new homes in Rome.

B. 1. When Ancus was king a stranger hearing of the power of Rome came thither.

2. When he had reached the Tiber an eagle took away his cap.

3. Then replacing the cap the bird flew away towards heaven.

4. The wife of the stranger seeing this said that the bird sent from heaven foretold good fortune.

5. She said that the cap being thus taken away and replaced her husband would attain a throne.

XV

Rules. *L. G.* § 301. Verbs of *commanding* (except iubeo, which takes infin.), *advising, persuading, begging* take the

subjunctive with ut in affirmative, ne in negative sentences.
'I advise you to do this', te moneo ut hoc facias : 'I ordered
you not to do this', tibi imperavi ne hoc faceres. Read
up § 148 and observe the sequence of tenses as in Ex. VII.
For the cases after these verbs see § 118.

A. 1. Tanaquil urged Tarquinius to go to the palace.

2. Ancus ordered him not to leave Rome.

3. He persuaded him to educate his sons.

4. When Ancus died Tanaquil begged the Romans to
create Tarquinius king.

5. Having thus attained the throne Tarquinius ordered
the people to go away.

B. 1. After collecting an army the king wished to
increase the number.

2. An augur being informed forbade Tarquinius to do
this.

3. The king said that he would not obey. 'Are you
so wise that you know my thoughts ? '

4. The augur thus questioned replied that he knew his
thoughts.

5. Tarquinius then ordered him to cut a stone with
a knife. The augur having done this the king decided
to obey.

XVI

Rules. *L. G.* § 60. Again read rules for interrogatives,
§ 292 for double interrogatives. § 387. After verbs of *fearing*, use ut or ne non with subj. in negative sentences, ne
in affirmative sentences. 'I fear that he will not come',
timeo ut veniat, timeo ne non veniat. 'I feared that he
would come', timebam ne veniret. Remember the sequence
of tenses. § 148.

A. 1. They feared that their men would not defeat the
enemy.

2. Do you not fear that the Sabines when routed will flee to the mountains ?

3. Shall we make peace or not ?

4. Did Tarquinius benefit the state or not ?

5. Will you not come home with me to-morrow ?

B. 1. The slaves seeing the fire feared that it would harm the boy.

2. Tanaquil ordered the slaves not to extinguish the fire.

3. She said to Tarquinius : ' Do you not see the flame ? Does it not foretell good fortune ? '

4. Were her words true or false ? Did the boy enjoy good fortune ?

5. Did the sons of Ancus murder Tarquinius, the Roman king, justly or not ?

XVII

Rules. *L. G.* § 283. Instead of ut, the relative **qui** may be used to express a purpose (**quo** being used in place of **ut** if the subordinate clause contains a comparative, § 365). The relative may be subject or object to its verb. See Ex. I. ' He sends ambassadors to (= who may) ask for peace', **mittit legatos qui (= ut) pacem petant.** ' He has few men to send ', **paucos habet quos mittat.** § 257. After comparatives ' than ' is translated by **quam**, in which case the moods and cases that follow must be the same as in the sentence that precedes, or the abl. of comparison, § 121 (c), may be used, but only when the things compared are in the nomin. or accus. **Caesar maior Pompeio, Caesar maior quam Pompeius, ferunt eum esse maiorem Pompeio, ferunt eum esse maiorem quam Pompeium.** With other cases quam must be used. **Facilius est mihi quam tibi** (not **te** without quam). **Pompei exercitus maior erat quam Caesaris** (not **Caesare** without quam).

A. 1. Tanaquil sent slaves to attend to the wound of the king.

2. The queen sends messengers to summon Servius.

3. She deceived the people in order that Servius might attain the throne more easily.

4. Servius was wiser than many of the Roman kings.

5. The death of Servius was more cruel than that of Ancus.

B. 1. When the king was dead Servius was stronger than the sons of Ancus.

2. It is agreed that Servius was wiser than Ancus.

3. It is clear that it was easier for Servius to seize the throne than for the sons of the king.

4. He increased the number of soldiers in order to have a stronger army.

5. He wished to have a strong army in order to lead it against the territory of his enemies.

XVIII

Rules. *L. G.* §§ 140-2. The word 'must' is translated in the passive voice by the gerundive, and may be followed by the agent in the dative (if the verb is one that governs the dat. a, ab is used with the abl. , 'we must go', nobis eundum est, i e. 'it must be gone by us'. If the Latin verb is followed by a direct object, 'we must defeat the enemy', the sentence is turned, hostes nobis vincendi sunt; but after verbs that take the dat., 'we must spare the enemy', hostibus a nobis parcendum est.

A. 1. A plan must be formed by us.

2. He must persuade his wife.

3. They said that they must kill Servius.

4. Armed men must enter the forum.

5. All citizens must help us that the king may be more easily defended.

B 1. Servius said that Tarquinius must leave the senate-house.

2. ' Do you dare to summon the senators to the senate-house ? '

3. In order to seize the throne Tarquinius saw that he must kill Servius.

4. Tullia seeing the body of her father ordered her slave to crush it with the wheels of the chariot.

5. The slave had to obey Tullia, but all men must confess that the crime was impious.

XIX

RULES. *L.G.* § 135. The gerunds are the cases of the infin. The accus. gerund is used after prep. ' born to rule ', natus ad regendum : the genit. ' desirous of ruling ', cupidus regendi : dat. ' devoted to ruling ', deditus regendo : abl. used as abl. of manner or with a prep. ' he was worn out by ruling ', fessus erat regendo. When the gerund is in the genit. or abl. it may govern a case, hostem vincendi causa, ' for the sake of . . . ' ; hostem fugando vicit, ' he won by routing the foe '. § 279. But when the gerund governs an object, it is more usual to put the noun into the case of the gerund, and to use the gerundive agreeing in gender, number, and case with the noun : natus ad regendos populos : cupidus regendi populi : deditus regendis populis, §§ 138, 139, and 279.

A. 1. Superbus was desirous of reigning.

2. By killing many senators he seized the throne.

3. By collecting an army he crushed his enemies.

4. He was desirous of weakening the senate.

5. This he did for the sake of strengthening his power.

B. 1. Superbus was devoted to increasing his kingdom.

2. And so he hoped by sending Sextus to Gabii to seize the town.

3. For the sake of carrying out this plan Sextus remained many months at Gabii.

4. By killing some Gabines and by banishing others he weakened the citizens.

5. It is agreed that no one was more useful for carrying out a treacherous plan than Sextus.

XX

Rules. *L. G.* § 200 (*b*). Indirect questions (which include very many that do not appear at first sight to be questions at all) may follow verbs of *asking, knowing, ignorance, considering, doubt, telling*, &c., the verb of the subordinate clause always being in the subjunctive. 'It is uncertain what he is doing', **incertum est quid agat.** 'I did not know where you were living', **nesciebam ubi habitares.** For the future subjunctive use the periphrastic conjugation, § 73. 'Tell me whether you will be present or not', **dic mihi utrum adfuturus sis necne.** See list of interrog. §§ 60 (*f*), 292-4.

A. 1. When the town was taken Tarquinius began to beautify Rome.

2. He did not understand what the omens portended.

3. It was uncertain whether the omens were favourable.

4. He sent messengers to Delphi to ask the god what could be done.

5. He doubted whether to send Brutus with his sons.

B. 1. It is uncertain whether all Romans thought that Brutus was foolish.

2. They wondered whether they should ask the oracle or not who should attain the throne.

3. No one knew to whom the throne was likely (=about) to come.

4. When they had heard the answer of the god they wondered which of the two would be king.

5. Brutus was wiser than they and understood what the oracle foretold.

RECAPITULATORY EXERCISES

The following are easy exercises for recapitulation. Try to think out in each sentence which is the rule to be applied.

I

1. Next year they marched into the territory of the enemy with a large army.

2. We said that we had been deceived by our friends.

3. He ordered the citizens to obey the laws of their country.

4. They have come from Alba and they will remain at Rome for many days.

5. Persuade the senators to call Servius king.

6. I did not know whether the sons of the king were going to help us or not.

7. Numa said that Egeria had not told him these things.

8. Will he come to help us in freeing the city?

9. Let them remain at home to receive us after the battle.

10. Our (men) having been overwhelmed by the great number of the enemy determined to leave the city.

II

1. The general having come to Rome informed the people of the victory.

2. Do you know that they have pitched their camp in our territory?

3. The Roman having separated the three Albans by fleeing decided to fight.

4. We must kill the enemy; we must spare our own people.

5. The Romans knew that the women of the Sabines would be carried away.

6. It is agreed that Tarpeia was bribed to receive the Sabines into the citadel.

7. Ask whether Tarpeia was bribed or not.

8. We ordered the ambassador to declare war on the Latins.

9. The soldiers were so many that they could not remain in the camp.

10. After the death of Romulus the throne was given to Numa, the wisest of the kings.

III

1. The women begged their husbands not to abandon their children to the enemy.

2. Let us make peace and return home without bloodshed.

3. The army of the Romans seemed to be larger than that of the Sabines.

4. Having left the camp, they took away the spoils with them.

5. Tullia feared that she would be punished for her crimes by the people.

6. We hoped to come to Ardea next day.

7. Lucretia killed herself with a knife which she had in her hand.

8. For many years the Greeks fought with the Trojans near Troy.

9. When Tarquin was in the camp, he was informed of the death of Lucretia.

10. You must fight with the enemy for your wives and children.

IV

1. Having spoken to me for many hours, the messenger at length left the camp.

2. Did you not think that the augur would be summoned by the king?

3. All the boys said that they did not understand what was being done.

4. Three men having been murdered by robbers were lying before the Senate-house.

5. Was Egeria, who gave advice to Numa, a woman or a goddess?

6. No one knew whether Romulus had returned to heaven or not.

7. The strangers were so angry that they did not stay with us on that day.

8. We, who hope to help you, will not flee.

9. Annoyed by the boys, they said that they would not come back.

10. They answered that this refuge had been opened for others, not for themselves.

V

1. The king must defeat the armies of the enemy.

2. The citizens urged the king to defend them against the enemy.

3. No one believed at that time that Brutus was wiser than the sons of the king.

4. You, who stain your hands with blood, are imitating the crimes of Tullia.

5. Servius, having been made king, formed the plan of fortifying the city with a wall.

6. The soldier, who had been wounded in the battle, feared that we should not attend to his wound.

7. Do you wish to go away, or have you decided to help me?

8. Having gone out of the house, we asked the messenger what had been foretold by the oracle.

9. Let us take an example from Numa; let us not attain to power by crime.

10. The augur having come into the palace said that the omens were not favourable.

ENGLISH-LATIN VOCABULARY

The grammar must be used in conjunction with the vocabulary for declining nouns and adjectives and for conjugating regular verbs.

Proper names are taken from the text and are to be found in the Proper Name vocabulary.

abandon, re-linquo, -līqui, -lictum. 3.

able (to be), possum, potui, posse.

about, dē.

acquit, absol-vo, -vi,-ūtum, 3.

admit, ac-cipio, -cēpi, -ceptum, 3.

advice, consili-um, -i, n.

after, post, *with* acc. *and as* adv.

against, contra, in w. acc.

agreed, it is, constat, 1 impers.

alarm, perturbo, 1.

all, omn-is, -e, adj.

allow, con-cēdo, -cessi, -cessum ; per-mitto, -mīsi, -missum, 3 (dat.).

already, iam, adv.

also, etiam.

ambassador, lēgāt-us, -i, m.

and, et, -que (suffixed to the word to which it belongs).

and so, itaque.

angry, īrāt-us, -a, -um, adj.

angry (to be), ir-ascor, -ātus, 8 dep. (*with* dat.).

announce, narro, 1.

annoy, vexo, 1.

answer, respon-deo, -di, -sum, 2.

answer, an, respons-um, -i, n.

appeal, prŏvoco, 1.

appease, plāco, 1.

approach, to, appropinquo, 1 (dat.); ag-gredior, -gressus, 3 dep.

arm, bracchi-um, -i, n.

armed, armātus, adj.

army, exercit-us, -ūs, m.

ash, cin-is, -eris, m.

ask, rogo, 1 ; pet-o, -īvi *or* -ii, -ītum, 3.

at, ad *with* acc. (*sometimes in with* abl.).

attain, ad-ipiscor, -eptus, 3 dep.

attend to, cūro, 1.

augur, aug-ur, -uris, m. and f.

avoid, vīto, 1.

band, man-us, -ūs, f.

banish, ex-pello, -puli, -pulsum, 3.

bank, rīp-a, -ae, f.

battle, pugn-a, -ae, f.

be, sum, fui, esse.

beautify, decoro, 1.
because of, propter (acc.).
before, ante, *with* acc. *and as*
adv.
beg, ōro, 1.
beg for, pet-o, -īvi *or* -ii,
-ītum, 3.
begin, in-cipio, -cōpi, -ce-
ptum, 3.
believe, crēd-o, -didi, -di-
tum, 3 (dat.).
benefit, prō-sum, -fui, -desse.
besides, praetereā.
bind, colligo, 1.
bird, av-is, -is, f.
blame, culpo, 1.
blood, sang-uis, -uinis, m.
bloodshed, sang-uis, -uinis,
m.
body, corp-us, -oris, n.
boldness, audāci-a, -ae, f.
born (to be), nascor, nātus,
3 dep.
both . . . and, et . . . et.
boy, pu-er, -eri, m.
brave, fort-is, -e, adj.
bravery, virt-ūs, -ūtis, f.
bribe, cor-rumpo, -rūpi, -ru-
ptum, 3.
bring, fero, tuli, lātum, also
of laws, bring in, intro-
duce ; dū-co, duxi, du-
ctum, 3.
bring up, ēduco, 1.
brother, frāt-er, -ris, m.
bury, sep-elio, -elīvi, -ultum,
4.
but, sed.
by, a, ab (*with* abl.).

call, appello, 1 ; voco, 1.
camp, castr-a, -ōrum, n. plur.
can, possum, potui, posse.
cap, pīle-us, -i, m.

capital, cap-ut, -itis, n.
capture, capio, cēpi, captum,
3.
carry, veho, vexi, vectum, 3 ;
porto, 1.
carry away, aufero, abstuli,
ablātum.
carry out, per-ficio, -fēci,
-fectum, 3.
cavalry, equit-es, -um, m.
plur.
champion,   prōpugnāt-or,
-ōris, m.
charge, concur-ro, -ri, -sum,
3.
chariot, curr-us, -ūs, m.
children, puer-i, -ōrum, m.
plur. ; līber-i, -ōrum, m.
plur. (only in relation to
their parents).
citadel, ar-x, -cis, f.
citizen, cīv-is, -is, c.
city, urb-s, -is, f.
clear, it is, liquet, 2 impers.
collect, col-ligo, -lēgi, -le-
ctum, 3 ; comparo, 1.
come, venio, vēni, ventum, 4.
confess, con-fiteor, -fessus, 2
dep.
country, pătri-a, -ae, f. ;
terr-a, -ae, f.
crafty, callidus, adj.
create, creo, 1.
crime, scel-us, -eris, n.
cruel, crūdēl-is, -e, adj.
crush, op-primo, -pressi,
-pressum, 3.
cry, clām-or, -ōris, m.
cut, disc-indo, -idi, -issum, 3.

dare, au-deo, -sus, 2 semi-
dep.
day, di-es, -ēi, m. and f. ; to-
day, hodiē, adv.

death, mor-s, -tis, f.
deceive, dē-cipio, -cēpi, -ceptum, 3.
decide, constit-uo, -ui, -ūtum, 3.
decide (a battle), dē-cerno, -crēvi, -crētum, 3, w. rem.
declare (war), in-dīco, -dixi, -dictum, 3.
defeat, vinco, vīci, victum, 3; supero, 1.
defend, dēfen-do, -di, -sum, 3.
deny, nego, 1.
desert, dēser-o, -ui, -tum, 3 ; re-linquo, -līqui, -lictum, 3.
desirous, cupid-us, -a, -um (gen.), adj.
destroy, dēl-eo, -ēvi, -ētum, 2.
devote myself to, me dē-do, -didi, -ditum (dat.).
die of, per-eo, -ii, -itum (with abl.) ; morior, mortuus, 3 dep.
discourse, collo-quor, -cūtus, 3 dep.
disease, morb-us, -i, m.
display, ostento, 1.
do, facio, fēci, factum, 3.
doubt, dubito, 1.
drag, traho, traxi, tractum, 3.
draw (a sword), stringo, strinxi, strictum, 3.

eager for, cupid-us, -a, -um (gen.), adj.
eagle, aquil-a, -ae, f.
earth, terr-a, -ae, f.
easily, facile.
easy, facil-is, -e, adj.
educate, ēduco, 1.
embrace, ampl-ector, -exus, 3 dep.
empty, vānus, adj.

enemy, host-is, -is, c., generally used in plur. ; inimīc-us, -i, m.
enjoy, fru-or, -itus, 3 dep., w. abl.
enter, in-eo, -īvi or -ii, -itum.
entertain, ac-cipio, -cēpi, -ceptum, 3.
escape, ef-fugio, -fūgi, -fugitum, 3.
every, omn-is, -e, adj.
example, exempl-um, -i, n.
extinguish, exstin-guo, -xi, -ctum, 3.

fail, dē-sum, -fui, -esse.
false, falsus, adj.
father, pat-er, -ris, m.
favourable, secundus, adj.
fear, tim-eo, -ui, 2.
feed, al-o, -ui, alitum (altum), 3.
fetter, vincul-um, -i, n.
fight, pugno, 1.
fill, com-pleo, -plēvi, -plētum, 2.
find, in-venio, -vēni, -ventum, 4.
fire, ign-is, -is, m.
first, at, prīmo, adv.
flame, flamm-a, -ae, f.
flee, fugio, fūgi, fugitum, 3.
fly away, āvolo, 1.
foe, host-is, -is, c., generally used in plur.
follow, se-quor, -cūtus, 3 dep.
foolish, stultus, adj.
for, prep. pro (abl.).
forbid, vet-o, -ui, -itum, 1.
forces, cōpi-ae, -ārum, f. plur.
foretell, praedī-co, -xi, -ctum, 3.
form (a plan), capio, cēpi, captum, 3.

fortify, mūnio, 4.
fortune, fortūn-a, -ae, f.
forum, for-um, -i, n.
found, con-do, -didi, -ditum,
3.
free, līber, adj.
free, to, lībero, 1
friend, amīc-us, -i, m.
from, a, ab (abl.); (= out of),
e, ex (abl.).

general, dux, ducis, c.
give, do, dedi, datum, 1.
go, eo, īvi or ii, itum.
go away, ab-eo, -īvi or -ii,
-itum.
go out, ex-eo, -īvi or -ii, -itum.
god, de-us, -i, m.
goddess, de-a, -ae, f.
good, bonus, adj.
great, magn-us, -a, -um, adj.
grief, luct-us, -ūs, m.

hand, man-us, -ūs, f.
happen, accid-o, -i, 3.
harm, noceo, 2, w. dat.
hastily, celeriter.
hate, ōdi, defective.
have, habeo, 2.
he, is, ea, id, pron.
hear of, to, audio, 4 (de,
with abl.).
heaven, cael-um, -i, n.
heavy, grav-is, -e, adj.
help, auxili-um, -i, n.
help, to, sub-venio, -vēni,
-ventum, 4 (dat.); ad-iuvo.
-iūvi, -iūtum, 1 (acc.).
her, see his.
here, hīc, adv.
high, altus, adj.
hill, coll-is, -is, m.
himself, see self.

his or her, su-us, -a, -um
(reflexive); or ēius.
home, dom-us, -ūs, f.; to
home, domum; at home,
domi.
hope, to, spēro, 1.
hundred, centum, num. adj.
husband, marīt-us, -i, m.

I, ego, me, mei, mihī, me.
imitate, imitor, 1 dep.
impious, impius, adj.
in, in, with acc. of motion,
with abl. of rest.
in order to, ut; in order
not to, nē.
increase, au-geo, -xi, -ctum, 2.
inform, certiōrem facio.
inform of, certiōrem facio do
(with abl.).
inhabit, habito, 1.
instead of, pro, w. abl.
into, in (with acc.).
its, su-us, -a, -um (reflexive);
ēius.

justly, iustē, adv.

kill, occī-do, -di, -sum, 3.
kind, benignus, adj.
king, rex, rēgis, m.
knife, cult-er, -ri, m.
know, scio, 4.
know, not, nescio, 4.

land, terr-a, -ae, f.
large, magnus, adj.
last, at, tandem.
law, lex, lēgis, f.
lead, dū-co, -xi, -ctum, 3.
leap over, tran-silio, -siluī
and -silīvi, 4.

leave, ex-eo, -īvi *or* -ii,
-itum (*with* abl.) ; re-
linquo, -līqui, -lictum, 3.
left, laevus, adj.
lest, nĕ.
lictor, lict-or, -ōris, m.
lie, iac-eo, -ui, 2.
life, vīt-a, -ae, f.
live, vīvo, vixi, victum, 3.
love, am-or, -ōris, m.

make, facio, fēci, factum, 3 ;
creo, 1.
man, hom-o, -inis, c. ; vir,
-i, m. ; his men, *often* su-i,
-ōrum, m. plur.
many, mult-i, -ae, -a, plur.
march, to, iter facio, fēci,
factum ; conten-do, -di,
-tum, 3.
master, domin-us, -i, m.
me, *see* I.
meet together, con-grĕdior,
-gressus, 3 dep.
messenger, nunti-us, -i, m.
month, mens-is, -is, m.
mother, māt-er, -ris, f.
mount, mountain, mon-s,
-tis, m.
much, mult-us, -a, um, adj.
murder, trucīdo, i.
my, meus, possess. adj.

name, nōm-en, -inis, n.
near, prope, *w.* acc.
nevertheless, tamen.
new, novus, adj.
news, nunti-us, -i, m. ; rēs,
rei, f.
next, poster-us, -a, -um, adj.
next day, postrīdiĕ.
no one, nēm-o, nullĭus (as
genit. of nēmo).

not, nōn ; in questions,
nonne.
now, nunc.
number, numer-us, -i, m.

obey, pāreo, 2 (dat.).
offer (sacrifices), facio, fēci,
factum, 3.
old (man), senex, senis ; adj.
vetus.
omen, ōm-en, -inis, n.
on, in (*with* abl. *or* acc.) ;
on account of, propter
(acc.) ; on behalf of, pro
(abl.).
one, unus, adj.
open, aper-io, -ui, -tum, 4.
opinion, sententi-a, -ae, f.
or, vel.
oracle, ōrācul-um, -i, n.
order, iubeo, iussi, iussum,
2 (acc.) ; impero, 1 (dat.).
other, ali-us, -a, -ud.
our, nost-er, -ra, -rum,
possess. adj.
overflow, ef-fundi, -fūsus, 3
passive, *w.* super (acc.).
overwhelm, op-primo, -pres-
si, -pressum, 3.
own, su-us, -a, -um (re-
flexive) ; ipsĭus, ipsōrum.

palace, rēgi-a, -ae, f.
peace, pax, pācis, f.
people, popul-us, -i, m. ;
multitud-o, -inis, f.
persuade, persuā-deo, -si,
-sum, 2 (dat.).
pestilence, pest-is, -is, f.
pitch, pōno, posui, positum,
3.
plan, consili-um, -i, n.
plot, consili-um, -i, n.
plunder, praed-a, -ae, f.

portend, porten-do, -di, -tum, 3.
power, potest-ās, -ātis, f.
practise, colo, colui, cultum, 8.
prefer, mālo, mālui, malle.
prepare, comparo, 1 ; paro, 1.
prepare (of a plan), capio, cēpi, captum, 3.
promise, to, prō-mitto, -mīsi, -missum, 3.
punish, pūnio, 4.

quarrel, rix-a, -ae, f.
queen, rēgīn-a, -ae, f.
question, interrogo, 1.
quickly, celeriter, adv.

race, gen-s, -tis, f.
reach, per-venio, -vēni, -ventum, 4.
receive, ac-cipio, -cēpi, -ceptum, 3.
refuge, asȳl-um, -i, n.
reign, regno, 1.
rejoice, gaudeo, gāvīsus, 2 semi-dep.
relate, narro, 1.
remain, man-eo, -si, -sum, 2.
replace, re-pōno, -posui, -positum, 3.
reply, respon-deo, -di, -sum, 2.
report, nuntio, 1 ; refero, rettuli, relātum.
resolve, constit-uo, -ui, -ūtum, 3.
rest, reliqui, reliquae, reliqua, plur.
return, red-eo, -īvi *or* -ii, -itum : rě-gredior, -gressus, 3 dep.
river, flūm-en, -inis, n.
robber, lătr-o, -ōnis, m..

rout, fugo, 1.
rule, rego, rexi, rectum, 3.
run, curro, cucurri, cursum, 3.

sacrifice, sacrifici-um, -i, n.
safe, tūtus, adj.
sail, nāvigo, 1.
sake of, for the, causā (*with* genit. which it follows).
same, īdem, eadem, idem.
say, dī-co, -xi, -ctum, 3.
say . . . not, nego, 1.
school, schol-a, -ae, f.
sea, mar-e, -is, n.
seal, signo, 1.
search, quae-ro, -sīvi *or* -sii, -sītum, 3.
see, video, vīdi, vīsum, 2 ; **seem,** videor.
seek for, pet-o, -īvi *or* -ii, -ītum, 3.
seek out, conquī-ro, -sīvi, -sītum. 3.
seize, occupo, 1.
self, ips-e, -a, -um.
senate, senāt-us, -ūs, m.
senate-house, cūri-a, -ae, f.
senator, senāt-or, -ōris, m.
send, mitto, mīsi, missum, 3.
separate, dissipo, 1.
set out, pro-ficiscor, -fectus, 3 dep.
shake, quatio, quassum, 3.
shepherd, past-or, -ōris, m.
shield, scūt-um, -i, n.
ship, nāv-is, -is, f.
short, brev-is, -e, adj.
shoulder, umer-us, -i, m.
sight, spectācul-um, -i, n.
sister, sor-or, -ōris, f.
slave, serv-us, -i, m.
slay, inter-ficio, -fēci, -fectum, 3.

small, parv-us, -a, -um, adj. ;
smaller, minor.
so, tam ; *but if* = therefore,
itaque.
so, and, itaque.
soldier, mil-es, -itis,m.; often
cōpi-ae, -ārum, f. plur.
so many, tot, adj., indecl.
some, nonnulli, m. plur.
some . . . others, alii . . . alii.
son, fīli-us, -i, m.
soon, mox.
spare, parco, peperci, par-
sum, 3 (dat.).
speak, dī-co, -xi, -ctum, 3 ;
lo-quor, -cūtus, 3 dep.
spoil, spoli-um, -i, n., usually
in plur.
stain, maculo, 1.
state, cīvit-ās, -ātis, f.
stay, stay at, maneo, mansi,
mansum, 2.
stone, lap-is, -idis, m.
story, fābul-a, -ae, f.
stranger, hosp-es, -itis, m.
strengthen, firmo, 1.
strike, per-cutio, -cussi, -cus-
sum, 3.
strong, validus, adj. :
= powerful, potens, adj.
summon, voco, 1.
sword, gladi-us, -i, m. ; ferrum, -i, n.

take, capio, cēpi, captum, 3 ;
take away, aufero, abstuli,
ablātum.
tell, dī-co, -xi, -ctum, 3 ;
narro, 1.
terrify, perturbo, 1.
territory, fīn-es, -ium, m.
plur.
than, quam.
that, ill-e, -a, -ud.

that, ut ; so that . . . not,
ut . . . non ; in order that
. . . not, nē.
thee, te.
their, theirs, su-us, -a, -um
(reflexive) ; eōrum.
themselves, *see* self.
then, tum, adv. deīnde.
there, ibī, adv.
therefore, itaque.
thing, rēs, rei, f.
think, arbitror, 1 dep. ; puto,
1.
this, hic, haec, hoc.
thither, eo.
thought, sententi-a, -ae, f.
threaten, minor, 1 dep.
three, trēs, tria.
throne, regn-um, -i, n.
throw, iacio, iēci, iactum, 3.
thunderbolt, fulm-en, -inis,
n.
thus, sīc, ita.
time, temp-us, -oris, n.
to, ad, in (acc.) ; but often =
in order to, which see.
to-morrow, cras.
towards, ad.
town, oppid-um, -i, n.
treacherous, perfidus, adj.
troops, cōpi-ae, -ārum, f.
plur.
true, vērus, adj.
two, duo, num. adj.

uncertain, incertus, adj.
understand, intell-ego, -exi,
-ectum, 3.
unhappy, miser, adj. ; in-
fēlix, adj.
unwilling, be, nō-lo, -lui, -lle.
urge, persuā-deo, -si, -sum, 2
(dat.) ; moneo, 2.

use, ūtor, ūsus, 3 dep. (abl.).
useful, ūtil-is, -e, adj.

vanish, ab-eo, -ivi or -ii, -itum.
victor, vict-or, -ōris, m.
victory, victōr-ia, -ae, f.

wall, mūr-us, -i, m.
war, bell-um, -i, n.
warfare, militi-a, -ae, f.
weaken, dēmin-uo, -ui, -ūtum, 3.
weep, fleo, flēvi, flētum, 2.
welcome, ac-cipio, -cēpi, -ceptum, 3.
what, qui, quae, quod, interrog. adj.
wheel, rot-a, -ae, f.
when, cum.
whether, num, ŭtrum.
whether...or, ŭtrum...an.
which, who, qui, quae, quod.
which of two, ut-er, -ra, -rum.
who, relat. qui, quae, quod.
who, interrog. quis, quid.

why, cūr.
wife, ux-or, -ōris, f.
willing, to be, volo, volui, velle.
win (a victory), reporto, 1.
winter, hiem-s, -is, f.
wise, prūden-s, -tis, adj.
wisely, prūdenter, adv.
wish, volo, volui, velle ; cupio, cupīvi, cupii, cupītum, 3.
with, cum (with abl.).
without, sine (abl.).
wolf, lup-a, -ae, f.
woman, muli-er, -eris, f.
wonder, mīror, 1 dep.
word, verb-um, -i, n.
world, orb-is'(-is, m.) terrārum (gen. f. plur.).
wound, vuln-us, -eris, n.
wound, to, vulnero, 1.

year, ann-us, -i, m.
you, tū, tē, tui, tibī, tē.
young man, iuven-is, -is, m.
your, tu-us, -a, -um ; vest-er, -ra, -rum, possess. adj.

— **B-C Publishers** have the following aphorisms available on Buttons. —

L0   **Latin:** The Basic Language.

L1   Lis litem parit. *(Anon. ARTES LATINAE)* **One lawsuit creates another.**

L2   Spem successus alit. *(Anon. ARTES LATINAE)* **Success feeds hope.**

L3   Dies dolorem minuit. *(Burton ARTES LATINAE)* **Time diminishes grief.**

L4   Necessitas non habet legem. *(St. Bernard? ARTES LATINAE)* **Necessity does not know any law.**

L5   Cucullus non facit monachum. *(Anon. ARTES LATINAE)* **The cowl does not make the monk.**

L6   Fides facit fidem. *(Anon. ARTES LATINAE)* **Trust creates more trust.**

L7   Ditat Deus. *(ARTES LATINAE)* **God enriches.**

L8   Principatus virum ostendit. *(Aristotle ARTES LATINAE)* **Leadership proves the man.**

L9   Stilus virum arguit. *(Anon. ARTES LATINAE)* **The pencil (or style) reveals the man. / You can tell what a man is by what he writes.**

L10   Injuria solvit amorem. *(Anon. ARTES LATINAE)* **Injury destroys love.**

L11   Amat victoria curam. *(Anon. ARTES LATINAE)* **Victory likes careful preparation.**

L12   Experientia docet. *(Tacitus ARTES LATINAE)* **Experience teaches.**

L13   Occasio facit furem. *(Medieval ARTES LATINAE)* **Opportunity makes a thief.**

L14   Gutta cavat lapidem. *(Ovid ARTES LATINAE)* **A drop hollows out the stone.**

L15   Regnat populus. *(Anon. ARTES LATINAE)* **The people rule.**

L16   Sors aspera monstrat amicum. *(Anon. ARTES LATINAE)* **Bitter fortune shows a friend.**

L17   Sermo mollis frangit iram. *(Anon. ARTES LATINAE)* **Soft speech dispels anger.**

L18   Flos unus non facit hortum. *(Anon. ARTES LATINAE)* **One flower does not make a garden.**

Through Buttons
Vivat Lingua Latina

L19   Semper avarus eget. *(Horace ARTES LATINAE)* **The miser is always in need.**

L20   Vanescit absens et novus intrat amor. *(Ovid ARTES LATINAE)* **The absent love vanishes and the new love enters.**

L21   Quis...bene celat amorem. *(Ovid. ARTES LATINAE)* **Who can successfully conceal love?**

L22   Homo proponit sed Deus disponit. *(Thomas a Kempis? ARTES LATINAE)* **Man proposes but God disposes.**

L23 Ex auricula asinum. *(Anon. Artes Latinae)* **One can recognize a donkey from his ear.**

L24 Nemo in amore videt. *(Propertius Artes Latinae)* **No one sees when he is in love.**

L25 Nulla regula sine exceptione. *(Anon. Artes Latinae)* **No rule without an exception.**

L26 Ex ungue leonem. *(Anon. Artes Latinae)* **From the claw we can recognize the lion.**

L27 Ubi bene, ibi patria. *(Anon. Artes Latinae)* **Where things are prosperous, there is my homeland.**

L28 Ignis non extinguitur igne. *(Anon. Artes Latinae)* **Fire is not extinguished by fire.**

L29 Amicus in necessitate probatur. *(Medieval Artes Latinae)* **A friend is proven in time of necessity.**

L30 In vino, in ira, in puero semper est veritas. *(Anon. Artes Latinae)* **Truth always exists in wine, in anger, and in a child.**

A Button for every occasion

L31 Dum feles dormit, mus gaudet. *(Anon. Artes Latinae)* **While a cat sleeps, the mouse rejoices.**

L32 Pro bono publico. *(Anon. Artes Latinae)* **For the public good.**

L33 Tempus fugit. *(Anon. Artes Latinae)* **Time flies.**

L34 Natura abhorret vacuum. *(Spinoza Artes Latinae)* **Nature abhors a vacuum.**

L35 Veritas odium parit. *(Burton Artes Latinae)* **Truth creates hatred.**

L36 Mala herba cito crescit. *(Anon. Artes Latinae)* **A weed grows quickly.**

L37 Nemo nisi vitio suo miser est. *(Seneca Artes Latinae)* **No one is unhappy except through his own fault.**

L38 Malum vas non frangitur. *(Anon. Artes Latinae)* **The bad vase does not get broken.**

L39 In mari aquam quaerit. *(Anon. Artes Latinae)* **He is looking for water in the ocean.**

L40 Ovem in fronte, vulpem in corde gerit. *(Anon. Artes Latinae)* **He acts like a sheep in his face but like a fox in his heart.**

L41 Omne ignotum pro magnifico est. *(Tacitus Artes Latinae)* **Everything unknown is considered to be magnificent.**

L42 Ubi est thesaurus tuus, ibi est et cor tuum. *(N.T. Artes Latinae)* **Where your treasure is, there is your heart also.**

THESE APHORISMS ARE AVAILABLE ON BUTTONS FROM BOLCHAZY-CARDUCCI PUBLISHERS

L43 Suaviter et fortiter. *(Motto Artes Latinae)* **Gently but firmly.**

L44 Simile simili gaudet. *(Medieval Artes Latinae)* **Like rejoices in like.**

L45 Virescit vulnere virtus. *(Motto Artes Latinae)* **Virtue grows powerful by wounds.**

L46 Crimine nemo caret. *(Anon. Artes Latinae)* **No one is free from accusation of wrong-doing.**

L47 Obsequium amicos, veritas odium parit. *(Terence Artes Latinae)* **Compliance makes friends, the truth creates hatred.**

L48 Felicitas multos habet amicos. *(Erasmus Artes Latinae)* **Prosperity has many friends.**

L49 Pauci sed boni. *(Anon. Artes Latinae)* **Few men, but good ones.**

L50 Post tenebras lux. *(Anon. Artes Latinae)* **After the darkness comes light.**

L51 Litterae non dant panem. *(Medieval Artes Latinae)* **Literature does not earn bread.**

L52 Mortui non dolent. *(Anon. Artes Latinae)* **The dead do not grieve.**

L53 Noscitur ex sociis. *(Anon. Artes Latinae)* **He is known from his companions.**

L54 Fabas indulcat fames. *(Anon. Artes Latinae)* **Hunger makes (even) beans pleasant.**

L55 De mortuis nil nisi bonum. *(Diogenes Laertius-translation Artes Latinae)* **About the dead nothing except good.**

L56 Natura...non facit saltum. *(Linnaeus? Artes Latinae)* **Nature does not make a sudden leap.**

L57 Laus alit artes. *(Seneca Artes Latinae)* **Praise nourishes the arts.**

L58 Necessitudo...etiam timidos fortes facit. *(Sallust Artes Latinae)* **Necessity makes even timid people brave.**

L59 Audaces Fortuna juvat timidosque repellit. *(Anon. Artes Latinae)* **Fortune aids the bold and repels the timid.**

L60 Urbes constituit aetas, hora dissolvit. *(Seneca Artes Latinae)* **A period of time builds up cities, a single hour destroys them.**

L61 Ignis aurum probat, miseria fortes viros. *(Anon. Artes Latinae)* **Fire tests gold, misfortune tests brave men.**

L62 In magno magni capiuntur flumine pisces. *(Anon. Artes Latinae)* **Large fish are captured in large rivers.**

L63 Modus omnibus in rebus. *(Plautus Artes Latinae)* **Moderation in all things.**

A different *Button* everyday!

L64 Vulpes pilum mutat, non mores. *(Suetonius Artes Latinae)* **The fox changes his skin but not his habits.**

L65 Ubi opes, ibi amici. *(Anon. Artes Latinae)* **Where wealth is, there friends are.**

L66 Impia sub dulci melle venena jacent. *(Ovid Artes Latinae)* **Wicked poisons lie under sweet honey.**

L67 Vulgus ex veritate pauca, ex opinione multa aestimat. *(Cicero Artes Latinae)* **The people judge a few things by their truth, and many by their opinion.**

L68 Labor omnia vincit. *(Vergil Artes Latinae)* **Labor conquers all things.**

L69 De minimis non curat lex. *(Legal Artes Latinae)* **The law does not care about trifles.**

L70 Vulpes non capitur muneribus. *(Medieval Artes Latinae)* **A fox is not caught by gifts.**

L71 Non redit unda fluens; non redit hora ruens. *(Medieval Artes Latinae)* **A flowing wave does not return; the rushing hour does not return.**

L72 Silent...leges inter arma. *(Cicero Artes Latinae)* **In time of war the laws are silent.**

L73 Pauca sed bona. *(Anon. Artes Latinae)* **Few things but good ones.**

Popularize Latin and Greek with Buttons

L74 Ratio omnia vincit. *(Anon. Artes Latinae)* **Reason conquers all things.**

L75 Variat omnia tempus. *(Anon. Artes Latinae)* **Time changes everything.**

L76 Verba movent, exempla trahunt. *(Anon. Artes Latinae)* **Words move people, examples draw them on.**

L77 Facta, non verba. *(Commonplace Artes Latinae)* **Deeds, not words.**

L78 Acta exteriora indicant interiora secreta. *(Legal Artes Latinae)* **Exterior acts indicate interior secrets.**

L79 Furor arma ministrat. *(Vergil Artes Latinae)* **Anger furnishes arms.**

L80 Fidus in adversis cognoscitur omnis amicus. *(Anon. Artes Latinae)* **A faithful friend is recognized in adverse circumstances.**

L81 Venter praecepta non audit. *(Seneca Artes Latinae)* **The stomach does not hear advice.**

L82 Acta deos numquam mortalia fallunt. *(Ovid Artes Latinae)* **Mortal acts never fool the gods.**

L83 Duobus litigantibus, tertius gaudet. *(Medieval Artes Latinae)* **When two people are quarreling, the third gets the profit.**

L84   Saepe summa ingenia in occulto latent. *(Plautus ARTES LATINAE)* **Often the greatest minds lie hidden.**

L85   Latrante uno, latrat statim et alter canis. *(Anon. ARTES LATINAE)* **When one dog barks, another dog immediately starts to bark.**

L86   Saepe tacens vocem verbaque vultus habet. *(Ovid ARTES LATINAE)* **Often a silent face has voice and words.**

L87   Crescit in adversis virtus. *(Lucan ARTES LATINAE)* **Courage increases in dangerous circumstances.**

L88   Jejunus venter non audit verba libenter. *(Medieval ARTES LATINAE)* **A hungry stomach does not gladly listen to speeches.**

L89   Verba dat omnis amor. *(Ovid ARTES LATINAE)* **Every lover deceives the person he loves.**

L90   Multum, non multa. *(Pliny the Younger ARTES LATINAE)* **Much, not many.**

L91   Ipsa scientia potestas est. *(Sir Francis Bacon? ARTES LATINAE)* **Knowledge itself is power.**

L92   Plumbum aurum fit. *(Petronius-adapted ARTES LATINAE)* **Lead becomes gold.**

L93   Nemo...patriam quia magna est amat, sed quia sua. *(Seneca ARTES LATINAE)* **No one loves his country because it is big but because it is his own.**

L94   Non est ad astra mollis e terris via. *(Seneca ARTES LATINAE)* **The trip from the earth to the stars is not an easy one.**

L95   Fames est optimus coquus. *(Anon. ARTES LATINAE)* **Hunger is the best cook.**

L96   Nemo malus felix. *(Juvenal ARTES LATINAE)* **No bad man is happy.**

L97   Res est forma fugax. *(Seneca ARTES LATINAE)* **Beauty is a fleeting thing.**

L98   Senectus ipsa est morbus. *(Terence ARTES LATINAE)* **Old age all by itself is a disease.**

L99   Nil sub sole novum. *(Ecclesiastes ARTES LATINAE)* **Nothing new under the sun.**

L100   Fortuna caeca est. *(Anon. ARTES LATINAE)* **Fortune is blind.**

L101   Rebus in humanis Regina Pecunia nauta est. *(Medieval ARTES LATINAE)* **In human affairs Queen Money is the one who runs the ship.**

L102   Amicus verus rara avis. *(Medieval ARTES LATINAE)* **A true friend is a rare bird.**

L103   Montani semper liberi. *(Anon. ARTES LATINAE)* **Mountaineers are always free.**

L104   Mors tua vita mea. *(Anon. ARTES LATINAE)* **Your death is my life.**

Remind your community
of the wisdom of the Ancients.

105   Vana est sine viribus ira. *(Anon. Artes Latinae)* **Anger without strength to enforce it is empty.**

106   Est certum praesens, sed sunt incerta futura. *(Medieval Artes Latinae)* **The present is certain, but the future is uncertain.**

107   Salus publica suprema lex. *(Legal Artes Latinae)* **The public safety is the supreme law.**

108   Longum iter est per praecepta, breve et efficax per exempla. *(Seneca Artes Latinae)* **The journey is long through advice, but short and efficient through examples.**

109   Maximum miraculum homo sapiens. *(Hermes Trismegistus Artes Latinae)* **A wise man is the greatest of all miracles.**

110   Varium et mutabile semper femina. *(Vergil Artes Latinae)* **Woman is always a fickle and changeable thing.**

111   Spiritus quidem promptus est, caro vero infirma. *(N.T. Artes Latinae)* **The spirit is willing but the flesh is weak.**

112   Laudatur ab his, culpatur ab illis. *(Horace Artes Latinae)* **He is praised by some, blamed by others.**

113   Nullis amor est sanabilis herbis. *(Ovid Artes Latinae)* **Love is curable by no herbs.**

114   Unus vir, nullus vir. *(Medieval Artes Latinae)* **One man, no man.**

115   Gutta cavat lapidem, consumitur anulus usu. *(Ovid Artes Latinae)* **Dropping water wears away a stone, a ring is worn out with use.**

116   In angustis amici boni apparent. *(Anon. Artes Latinae)* **Good friends appear in difficulties.**

117   Simul et dictum et factum. *(Anon. Artes Latinae)* **At once said and done.**

118   Forma viros neglecta decet. *(Ovid Artes Latinae)* **A careless appearance is suitable for men.**

119   Qui tenet anguillam per caudam non habet illam. *(Medieval Artes Latinae)* **Who holds an eel by the tail does not (really) hold him.**

120   Nihil est...simul et inventum et perfectum. *(Cicero Artes Latinae)* **Nothing is at once discovered and perfected.**

121   Saxum volutum non obducitur musco. *(Anon. Artes Latinae)* **A rolling stone is not covered with moss.**

122   Fumum fugiens in ignem incidit. *(Medieval Artes Latinae)* **Fleeing smoke, he falls into the fire.**

123   Ex pede Herculem. *(Anon. Artes Latinae)* **From his foot we can recognize Hercules.**

124   Finis coronat opus. *(Medieval Artes Latinae)* **The end crowns the work.**

125   Leonem mortuum et catuli mordent. *(Medieval Artes Latinae)* **Even puppies bite a dead lion.**

L126 Multa docet fames. *(Anon. ARTES LATINAE)* **Hunger teaches us much.**

L127 Vincit omnia veritas. *(Anon. ARTES LATINAE)* **Truth conquers all.**

L128 Nemo sua sorte contentus. *(Anon. ARTES LATINAE)* **No one is content w** his lot.

L129 Quis pauper? Avarus. *(Pseudo-Ausonius ARTES LATINAE)* **Who is the p** man? The miser.

L130 Omne initium est difficile. *(Anon. ARTES LATINAE)* **Every beginning is difficu**

L131 Mea anima est tamquam tabula rasa. *(Renaissance ARTES LATINAE)* **My mi** is like a clean tablet.

L132 Jus summum saepe summa est malitia. *(Terence ARTES LATINAE)* **T** highest law is often the highest evil.

L133 Se damnat judex, innocentem qui opprimit. *(Publilius Syrus ARTES LATIN* The judge who punishes an innocent man condemns himself.

L134 Male secum agit aeger, medicum qui heredem facit. *(Publilius Syr ARTES LATINAE)* **The sick man who makes his doctor his heir does hims** a disservice.

L135 Spina etiam grata est, ex qua spectatur rosa. *(Publilius Syrus ARTES LATIN* Even a thorn bush is pleasant, from which a rose is seen.

L136 Ubi judicat qui accusat, vis, non lex, valet. *(Publilius Syrus ARTES LATIN* Where the person who accuses is (also) the person who judges, violence, n law, prevails.

L137 Damnant quod non intellegunt. *(Anon. ARTES LATINAE)* **They condemn wh** they do not understand.

L138 Stultus nil celat: quod habet sub corde revelat. *(Medieval ARTES LATIN* The stupid person conceals nothing: he reveals what he has in his heart.

L139 Non bene olet qui bene semper olet. *(Martial ARTES LATINAE)* **A perso** does not smell good who always smells good.

L140 Qui capit uxorem, litem capit atque dolorem. *(Medieval ARTES LATIN* Who takes a wife, takes trouble and strife.

L141 Dat virtus quod forma negat. *(Medieval ARTES LATINAE)* **Virtue gives wh** beauty denies.

L142 Qui parce seminat, parce et metit. *(N.T. ARTES LATINAE)* **Who sow** sparingly also reaps sparingly.

With these Buttons
you can get the whole community
excited about Latin or Greek!

---

143 Suum cuique pulchrum est. *(Cicero* ARTES LATINAE*)* **One's own seems handsome to each person.**

144 Inopiae desunt multa; avaritiae omnia. *(Publilius Syrus* ARTES LATINAE*)* **Many things are lacking to poverty; everything is lacking to greed.**

145 Formicae grata est formica, cicada cicadae. *(Theocritus* ARTES LATINAE*)* **An ant is pleasing to an ant, and a grasshopper to another grasshopper.**

146 Nihil difficile amanti. *(Cicero* ARTES LATINAE*)* **Nothing is difficult for the lover.**

147 Nihil...semper floret: aetas succedit aetati. *(Cicero* ARTES LATINAE*)* **Nothing flourishes forever: one generation succeeds another generation.**

148 Summa sedes non capit duos. *(Anon.* ARTES LATINAE*)* **The highest position does not hold two people.**

149 Meus mihi, suus cuique est carus. *(Plautus* ARTES LATINAE*)* **Who is mine is dear to me, who is someone else's is dear to him.**

150 Adulatio quam similis est amicitiae! *(Seneca* ARTES LATINAE*)* **How similar to friendship is flattery!**

151 Magnas inter opes inops. *(Horace* ARTES LATINAE*)* **Poor in the midst of great riches.**

152 Dictum sapienti sat est. *(Plautus* ARTES LATINAE*)* **A word to the wise is enough.**

153 Quot homines, tot sententiae; suus cuique mos. *(Terence* ARTES LATINAE*)* **There are as many opinions as there are men; each one has his own way of doing things.**

154 Sero dat qui roganti dat. *(Anon.* ARTES LATINAE*)* **He gives late who gives to one who asks.**

155 Mendaci, neque cum vera dicit, creditur. *(Cicero-adapted* ARTES LATINAE*)* **Belief is not given to a liar even when he tells the truth.**

156 Quod nimis miseri volunt, hoc facile credunt. *(Seneca* ARTES LATINAE*)* **What unhappy people want too much, this they easily believe.**

157 Mors omnibus instat. *(Grave inscription* ARTES LATINAE*)* **Death threatens all.**

158 Solitudo placet Musis, urbs est inimica poetis. *(Petrarch?* ARTES LATINAE*)* **Solitude pleases the Muses, the city is unfriendly for poets.**

159 Sol omnibus lucet. *(Petronius* ARTES LATINAE*)* **The sun shines upon us all.**

160 Puris omnia pura. *(N.T.* ARTES LATINAE*)* **To the pure all things are pure.**

161 Alia aliis placent. *(Anon.* ARTES LATINAE*)* **Different things please different people.**

162 Nihil amantibus durum est. *(St. Jerome* ARTES LATINAE*)* **Nothing is difficult for lovers.**

163 Fortuna favet fatuis. *(Anon.* ARTES LATINAE*)* **Fortune favors the stupid.**

164 Ne Juppiter quidem omnibus placet. *(Theognis* ARTES LATINAE*)* **Not even Jupiter is pleasing to everyone.**

165 Qui totum vult, totum perdit. *(Anon.* ARTES LATINAE*)* **Who wants all, loses all.**

L166 Qualis pater, talis filius. *(Anon. ARTES LATINAE)* **As the father is so is the s**

L167 Quot servi tot hostes. *(Festus? ARTES LATINAE)* **There are as many enemies there are slaves.**

L168 Equi donati dentes non inspiciuntur. *(St. Jerome ARTES LATINAE)* **Peop do not look at the teeth of a horse which is given to them.**

L169 Sic transit gloria mundi. *(Anon. ARTES LATINAE)* **Thus passes the glory the world.**

L170 Ignorantia legis neminem excusat. *(Legal ARTES LATINAE)* **Ignorance of t law excuses no one.**

L171 In casu extremae necessitatis omnia sunt communia. *(Legal ART LATINAE)* **In case of extreme necessity all things are in common.**

L172 Salus populi suprema lex. *(Legal ARTES LATINAE)* **The safety of the people the supreme law.**

L173 In nomine Domini incipit omne malum. *(Anon. ARTES LATINAE)* **Every e begins in the name of the Lord.**

L174 Vox populi vox Dei. *(Commonplace ARTES LATINAE)* **The voice of the people the voice of God.**

L175 Calamitas virtutis occasio est. *(Seneca ARTES LATINAE)* **Disaster is t opportunity for bravery.**

L176 Ira initium insaniae. *(Ennius-adapted ARTES LATINAE)* **Anger is the beginnir of insanity.**

L177 Externus hostis maximum in urbe concordiae vinculum. *(Anon. ART LATINAE)* **An enemy outside the city is the greatest bond of concord inside the cit**

L178 Omnis ars naturae imitatio est. *(Seneca ARTES LATINAE)* **All art is an imit tion of nature.**

L179 Qui debet, limen creditoris non amat. *(Publilius Syrus ARTES LATINAE)* **Th person who owes does not like the threshold of the person he owes money t**

L180 Amicus animae dimidium. *(Austin ARTES LATINAE)* **A friend is the half one's soul.**

L181 Tot mundi superstitiones quot caelo stellae. *(Burton ARTES LATINA There are as many superstitions in the world as there are stars in the sky.**

L182 Perjuria ridet amantum Juppiter. *(Lygdamus ARTES LATINAE)* **Jupiter laugh at the lies of lovers.**

L183 Repetitio est mater studiorum. *(Anon. ARTES LATINAE)* **Repetition is th mother of studies.**

L184 Bis dat qui cito dat. *(Alciatus? ARTES LATINAE)* **Who gives quickly gives twice**

L185 Maximum remedium irae mora est. *(Seneca ARTES LATINAE)* **Delay is th best remedy for anger.**

L186 Mors janua vitae. *(Anon. ARTES LATINAE)* **Death is the gateway to life.**

L187 Errare est humanum. *(Anon. ARTES LATINAE)* **To err is human.**

88 Ars est celare artem. *(Anon. ARTES LATINAE)* **It is the function of art to conceal art.**

89 Amare simul et sapere ipsi Jovi non datur. *(Anon. ARTES LATINAE)* **The ability to love and be wise at the same time is not given to Jupiter himself.**

90 Qui tacet consentire videtur. *(Legal ARTES LATINAE)* **Who is silent appears to give consent.**

91 Fraus est celare fraudem. *(Anon. ARTES LATINAE)* **It is dishonest to conceal dishonesty.**

92 Judicis est jus dicere, non dare. *(Legal ARTES LATINAE)* **It is the duty of the judge to explain the law, not to make it.**

93 Cum...docemus, discimus. *(Sergius ARTES LATINAE)* **While we teach, we learn.**

94 Dum spiro, spero. *(Motto ARTES LATINAE)* **While I breath, I hope.**

95 Homo sum; humani nil a me alienum puto. *(Terence ARTES LATINAE)* **I am a man; I consider nothing human alien to me.**

96 Sum quod eris. *(Grave inscription ARTES LATINAE)* **I am what you will be.**

97 Panem et circenses. *(Juvenal ARTES LATINAE)* **Bread and circuses.**

98 Hodie, non cras. *(Motto ARTES LATINAE)* **Today, not tomorrow.**

99 Magna est veritas et praevalebit. *(Anon. ARTES LATINAE)* **Great is truth and it will prevail.**

00 Ego sum rex Romanus et supra grammaticam. *(King Sigismund the First? ARTES LATINAE)* **I am a Roman king and above grammar.**

01 Neminem pecunia divitem fecit. *(Seneca ARTES LATINAE)* **Money has made no one rich.**

02 Verus amor nullum novit habere modum. *(Propertius ARTES LATINAE)* **True love does not know how to have moderation.**

03 Suaviter in modo, firmiter in re. *(Motto ARTES LATINAE)* **Gentle in how we do it, firm in what we do.**

04 Graecia capta ferum victorem cepit. *(Horace ARTES LATINAE)* **Conquered Greece captured her savage victor.**

05 Qui sibi non parcit, mihi vel tibi quo modo parcet? *(Medieval ARTES LATINAE)* **How will he spare either you or me, who does not spare himself?**

06 Astra inclinant sed non cogunt. *(Anon. ARTES LATINAE)* **The stars influence us but do not compel us.**

07 Inopem me copia fecit. *(Ovid ARTES LATINAE)* **Prosperity has made me poor.**

08 Faber est suae quisque fortunae. *(Appius Claudius Caecus ARTES LATINAE)* **Each person is the creator of his own fortune.**

09 Non omne quod nitet aurum est. *(Anon. ARTES LATINAE)* **Not everything which shines is gold.**

10 Cum grano salis. *(Anon. ARTES LATINAE)* **With a grain of salt.**

L211   Mali principii malus finis. *(Anon. ARTES LATINAE)* **A bad end to a b** **beginning.**

L212   Amicitia pares aut accipit aut facit. *(Aristotle ARTES LATINAE)* **Friendsh either accepts equals or makes them equals.**

L213   Aequat omnes cinis. *(Seneca ARTES LATINAE)* **Death makes everyone equa**

L214   Jus superat vires. *(Anon. ARTES LATINAE)* **Right overcomes might.**

L215   Abusus non tollit usus. *(Legal ARTES LATINAE)* **Abuse does not take away t right to use.**

L216   In pace leones, in proelio cervi. *(Tertullian ARTES LATINAE)* **They are lions times of peace and deer in battle.**

L217   Vestis virum reddit. *(Medieval ARTES LATINAE)* **Clothes make the man.**

L218   Manus manum lavat. *(Petronius ARTES LATINAE)* **(One) hand washes (anoth hand.**

L219   Non quaerit aeger medicum eloquentem. *(Seneca? ARTES LATINAE)* **A si person doesn't seek an eloquent doctor.**

L220   Mens sana in corpore sano. *(Juvenal ARTES LATINAE)* **A sound mind in sound body.**

L221   Aquila non capit muscas. *(Anon. ARTES LATINAE)* **An eagle does not catch flie**

L222   Religio deos colit, superstitio violat. *(Seneca ARTES LATINAE)* **Religic honors the gods, superstition violates them.**

L223   Ars longa, vita brevis. *(Hippocrates-translation ARTES LATINAE)* **Art is long, li is short.**

L224   Ira furor brevis est. *(Horace ARTES LATINAE)* **Anger is a short madness.**

L225   Nemo liber est qui corpori servit. *(Seneca ARTES LATINAE)* **No one is fre who is a slave to his body.**

L226   Vultus index animi. *(Anon. ARTES LATINAE)* **The face is the betrayer of the min**

L227   Cogito, ergo sum. *(Descartes? ARTES LATINAE)* **I think, therefore I am.**

L228   Sed quis custodiet ipsos custodes? *(Juvenal ARTES LATINAE)* **But who w watch the custodians themselves?**

L229   Veritas vos liberabit. *(N.T. ARTES LATINAE)* **The truth will set you free.**

L230   Primus in orbe deos fecit timor. *(Statius ARTES LATINAE)* **Fear first mad gods in the world.**

L231   Lusisti satis, edisti satis atque bibisti: Tempus abire tibi est. *(Horac ARTES LATINAE)* **You have played enough; you have eaten and drunk enough; it time for you to depart.**

L232   Veni, vidi, vici. *(Suetonius ARTES LATINAE)* **I came, I saw, I conquered.**

L233   Non sum ego qui fueram: mutat via longa puellas, / Quantus i exigui tempore fugit amor! *(Propertius ARTES LATINAE)* **I am not the person was: a long journey changes girls. How great a love fled in a short time!**

---

34 Duos qui sequitur lepores neutrum capit. *(Medieval ARTES LATINAE)* **He who chases two rabbits catches neither.**

35 Nemo...regere potest nisi qui et regi. *(Seneca ARTES LATINAE)* **No one can rule except he who can also be ruled.**

36 Dulce et decorum est pro patria mori. *(Horace ARTES LATINAE)* **It is sweet and fitting to die for one's country.**

37 Edamus, bibamus, gaudeamus; post mortem nulla voluptas. *(Anon. ARTES LATINAE)* **Let us eat, drink, and be merry; after death there is no pleasure.**

38 Fiat justitia, ruat caelum. *(Legal ARTES LATINAE)* **Let justice be done even though heaven may fall.**

39 Omnia vincit Amor; et nos cedamus Amori. *(Vergil ARTES LATINAE)* **Love conquers all; let us, too, yield to Love.**

40 Qui desiderat pacem praeparet bellum. *(Vegetius ARTES LATINAE)* **Who wishes peace should prepare for war.**

41 Aut bibat aut abeat. *(Cicero ARTES LATINAE)* **(A person) should either drink or get out.**

42 Non ut edam vivo, sed ut vivam edo. *(Quintilian ARTES LATINAE)* **I do not live to eat, but I eat to live.**

43 Frangar, non flectar. *(Motto ARTES LATINAE)* **I'll break but I will not bend.**

44 Trahimur omnes studio laudis. *(Cicero ARTES LATINAE)* **We are all impelled by a desire for praise.**

45 Video meliora proboque, deteriora sequor. *(Ovid ARTES LATINAE)* **I see and approve the better things, (but) I follow the worse ones.**

46 Audi, vide, tace, si vis vivere in pace. *(Medieval ARTES LATINAE)* **Listen, look, and be quiet if you wish to live in peace.**

47 Divide et impera. *(Anon. ARTES LATINAE)* **Divide and rule.**

48 Si foret in terris, rideret Democritus. *(Horace ARTES LATINAE)* **If Democritus were on earth (today), he would laugh.**

49 Quod licet Jovi non licet bovi. *(Anon. ARTES LATINAE)* **What is permitted to Jupiter (to do) is not permitted to the ox.**

50 Spectatum veniunt; veniunt spectentur ut ipsae. *(Ovid ARTES LATINAE)* **They come to see; they (also) come so that they themselves may be seen.**

51 Tantum religio potuit suadere malorum. *(Lucretius)* **Such great evils religion (superstition) could inspire.**

> # Buttons are Fun,
> ## Educational, Thought Provoking

The following are from a new textbook:

Ovid With Love (Selections from ARS AMATORIA, Books I and II).
ed. Paul Murgatroyd.

Bolchazy-Carducci Publishers.   Examination copy......$4.00.

"Selected but not Expurgated."

L252   Arte regendus amor. *(Ovid A.A 1.4)* **By skill must love be guided.**

L253   Et fora conveniunt amori. *(Ovid A.A. 1.79)* **Even the law-courts are suitable for love.**

L254   Utque viro furtiva venus, sic grata puellae. *(Ovid A.A. 1.275)* **And stolen love is pleasant to a man, so is it also to a woman.**

L255   Audentem Forsque Venusque juvat. *(Ovid A.A. 1.608)* **Chance and Venus help the brave.**

L256   Expedit esse deos. *(Ovid A.A. 1.637)* **It is expedient there should be gods.**

L257   Lacrimis adamanta movebis. *(Ovid A.A. 1.659)* **With tears you can melt iron.**

L258   Grata est vis ista puellis. *(Ovid A.A. 1.673)* **Women like you to use force.**

L259   Ut ameris, amabilis esto. *(Ovid. A.A. 2.107)* **That you may be loved, be lovable.**

L260   Forma bonum fragile est. *(Ovid A.A. 2.113)* **A frail advantage is beauty.**

L261   Dulcibus est verbis mollis alendus amor. *(Ovid. A.A. 2.152)* **With soft words must love be fostered.**

L262   Amor odit inertes. *(Ovid A.A. 2.229)* **Love hates the sluggish.**

L263   Militiae species amor est. *(Ovid A.A. 2.233)* **Love is a kind of warfare.**

L264   Si latet ars, prodest. *(Ovid. A.A. 2.313)* **Art if hidden, avails.**

L265   Non est veneris properanda voluptas. *(Ovid A.A. 2.717)* **Love's bliss must not be hastened.**

L266   Tum plena voluptas, cum pariter victi femina virque jacent. *(Ovid A. 2.727)* **Then is pleasure full, when man and woman lie vanquished both together.**

L267   Naso Magister Erat. *(Ovid A.A. 2.744)* **Naso (Ovid) was my Master.**

Bolchazy-Carducci Publishers have brought out a new textbook:

Phormio: A Comedy by Terence
ed. Elaine M. Coury.

This textbook is unique for it contains the reproduction of the entire fourth century Manuscript of *Phormio* together with facing transcription.

Examination Copy......$3.00

L268   Montes auri pollicens. *(Ter. PHORMIO - 68)* **Promising mountains of gold.**

L269   Fortes fortuna adjuvat. *(Ter. PHORMIO - 203)* **Fortune favors the brave.**

L270   Prima coitio est acerrima. *(Ter. PHORMIO - 346)* **The first attack's the fiercest.**

L271   Quot homines, tot sententiae. *(Ter. PHORMIO - 454)* **There are as many opinions as there are people.**

L272   Ah! dictum sapienti sat est. *(Ter. PHORMIO - 541)* **A word to the wise is sufficient.**

L273   Senectus ipsa morbus est. *(Ter. PHORMIO - 575)* **Old age itself is a sickness.**

L274 Vivamus mea Lesbia, atque amemus. *(Catullus 5.1)* **Let's live it up, Lesbia, and make love.**

L275 Da mihi basia mille. *(Catullus 5.7)* **Kiss me with a thousand kisses.**

G0 **Latin & Greek:** The Basic Languages.

G1 We are all Greeks. Our laws, our literature, our religion, our art, have their root in Greece. *(Shelley).*

G2 Εἷς ἀνὴρ οὐδεὶς ἀνήρ. *(Anonymous).* **One man no man.**

G3 Πόνος γάρ, ὡς λέγουσιν, εὐκλείας Πατήρ. *(Euripides, fragment).* **Toil, so they say, is the father fame.**

G4 οἱ γὰρ πόνοι τίκτουσι τὴν εὐανδρίαν. *(Euripides, fragment).* **Labor begets manhood.**

G5 πᾶν δένδρον ἀγαθὸν καρποὺς καλοὺς ποιεῖ. *(St. Matthew, VII. 17).* **Every good tree bringeth forth good fruit.**

G6 ἀρχὴ δέ τοι ἥμισυ παντός. *(Anon.)* **Well begun is half done.**

G7 σκηνὴ πᾶς ὁ βίος. *(Anon.)* **All the world's a stage.**

G8 λύπης ἰατρός ἐστιν ἀνθρώποις λόγος. *(Menander, fragment).* **In reason men find a physician for their grief.**

G9 Ἔργον δ’ οὐδὲν ὄνειδος, ἀεργίη δέ τ’ ὄνειδος. *(Hesiod, Works and Days, 311).* **Work is no disgrace, but idleness is.**

G10 Καλόν ἡσυχία. *(Periander).* **Leisure is a fine thing.**

G11 Ὅ τι καλὸν φιλον ἀεί. *(Euripides, Bacchae, 881).* **A thing of beauty is a joy forever.**

G12 Σοφῷ γὰρ αἰσχρὸν ἐξαμαρτάνειν. *(Aeschylus, Prometheus, 1039).* **'Tis shameful for a wise man to make mistakes.**

G13 Ὦ ταὶ λιπαραὶ καὶ ἰοστέφανοι καὶ ἀοίδιμοι, Ἑλλάδος ἔρεισμα, κλειναὶ Ἀθῆναι. *(Pindar, fragment).* **City of light, with thy violet crown, beloved of the poets, Thou art the bulwark of Greece; Athens, thy fame is for ay.**

G14 "Ετερος γὰρ αὐτὸς ὁ φίλος ἐστίν. *(Aristotle, Nicomachean Ethics, IX. 9. 10, 1170 B)*. **A friend is another self.**

G15 Σπεῦδε βραδέως. *(Suetonius, Augustus, 25)*. **Make haste slowly.**

G16 Θάλαττα, θάλαττα. *(Xenophon, Anabasis, IV. 7. 24)*. **The sea, the sea.**

G17 Ἀγαπήσεις τὸν πλησίον σου ὡς σαυτόν. *(St. Matthew, XIX. 19)*. **Thou shalt love thy neighbor as thyself.**

G18 "Αγροικός εἰμι· τὴν σκάφην σκάφην λέγω. *(Anon.)* **I am from the country; I call a spade a spade.**

G19 Δέσποινα γὰρ γέροντι νυμφίῳ γυνή. *(Euripides, fragment)*. **An old man's bride, an old man's boss.**

G20 "Αριστον μὲν ὕδωρ. *(Pindar, Olympian, I. 1)*. **Water is best.**

G21 Αἱ δεύτεραί πως φροντίδες σοφώτεραι. *(Euripides, Hippolytus, 436)*. **The sober second thought.**

G22 Ἐλπὶς ἐν ἀνθρώποις μούνη θεὸς ἐσθλὴ ἔνεστιν. *(Theognis, 1135)*. **Hope is man's one good deity.**

G23 Πάντων χρημάτων μέτρον ἄνθρωπος. *(Protagoras)*. **Man is the measure of all things.**

G24 Φιλεῖ δὲ τῷ κάμνοντι συσπεύδειν θεός. *(Aeschylus, fragment)*. **God helps him who helps himself.**

G25 Ἀνάγκᾳ δ' οὐδὲ θεοὶ μάχονται. *(Simonides)*. **Not even gods fight against necessity.**

G26 "Αρχε πρῶτον μαθὼν ἄρχεσθαι. *(Solon, as quoted by Diogenes Laertius, I. 60)*. **He who rules must first obey.**

G27 Χαλεπὸν τὸ ποιεῖν, τὸ δὲ κελεῦσαι ῥάδιον. *(Philemon, fragment)*. **Commanding is easy, but performance is hard.**

G28 Δὶς ἐξαμαρτεῖν ταὐτὸν οὐκ ἀνδρὸς σοφοῦ. *(Menander, fragment)*. **To make the same slip twice is not (the part) of a wise man.**

G29 Μέτρον ἄριστον. *(Diogenes Laertius, I. 93)*. **Moderation is best.**

G30 Γηράσκω δ' ἀεὶ πολλὰ διδασκόμενος. *(Solon)*. **The older I grow, the more I learn.**

G31 ΝΙΨΟΝΑΝΟΜΗΜΑΜΗΜΟΝΑΝΟΨΙΝ *(On Hagia Sophia)*. **Wash your sins, not only your face.**

G32 Τίς δὲ βίος, τί δὲ τερπνὸν ἄτερ χρυσῆς Ἀφροδίτης; *(Mimnermus)*. **What life, what joy without golden Aphrodite?**

G33 Μᾶλλον ἀ-δικεῖσθαι ἢ ἀ-δικεῖν. *(Plato, Gorgias, 469)*. **It is better to suffer harm than to do harm.**

G34 "Ον οἱ θεοὶ φιλοῦσιν ἀποθνήσκει νέος. *(Menander, fragment)*. **Whom the gods love dies young.**

G35 Χρήματα γὰρ ψυχὴ πέλεται δειλοῖσι βροτοῖσι. *(Hesiod, Works and Days, 686)*. **Money is the soul of craven men.**

G36 Τὸν καλὸν ἀγῶνα ἠγώνισμαι. *(II Timothy, IV. 7)*. **I have fought a good fight.**

G37 Κακῆς ἀπ' ἀρχῆς γίγνεται τέλος κακόν. *(Euripides, fragment).* **A bad start means a bad finish.**

G38 Οὐ πολλὰ ἀλλὰ πολύ *(Anon.)* **Not quantity but quality.**

G39 Χαλεπὸν τὸ μὴ φιλῆσαι. *(Anacreontic).* **'Tis hard not to love.**

G40 Χαλεπὸν δὲ καὶ φιλῆσαι. *(Anacreontic).* **And hard as well to love.**

G41 Φιλαργυρία μητρόπολις πάντων τῶν κακῶν. *(Diogenes Laertius, VI. 50).* **The love of money is the root of all evil.**

G42 Μελέτη τὸ πᾶν. *(Diogenes Laertius, I. 99).* **Practice makes perfect.**

G43 Οὐδὲ τεθνᾶσι θανόντες. *(Simonides).* **Though dead, they are not dead.**

G44 Οὐδὲν γλύκιον ἧς πατρίδος. *(Anon.)* **Naught is sweeter than one's native land.**

G45 Μὴ κρίνετε ἵνα μὴ κριθῆτε. *(St. Matthew, VII. 2).* **Judge not that ye be not judged.**

Through Buttons
Vivat Lingua Graeca

G46 Καιρὸς δ' ἐπὶ πᾶσιν ἄριστος. *(Hesiod, Works and Days, 694).* **Everything in season.**

G47 Εὕρηκα. *(Archimedes).* **I have it. I have found.**

G48 Τὸ νικᾶν αὐτὸν αὑτὸν πασῶν νικῶν πρώτη τε καὶ ἀρίστη. *(Plato, Laws, 626 E).* **Self-mastery is the first and noblest victory of all.**

G49 λαμπάδια ἔχοντες διαδώσουσιν ἀλλήλοις. *(Plato, Republic, I. 321 A)* **Having torches, they will pass them to each other.**

G50 Φιλοσοφία Βίου Κυβερνήτης. *(Anon.)* **Philosophy the Guide of Life.**

G51 Ζητῶ γὰρ τὴν ἀλήθειαν, ὑφ' ἧς οὐδεὶς πώποτε ἐβλάβη. *(Marcus Aurelius, Meditations, VI. 21).* **For I seek the truth, by which no man was ever harmed.**

G52 Τῷ σοφῷ ξένον οὐδέν. *(Antisthenes, as quoted by Diogenes Laertius, VI. 12).* **To the wise nothing is foreign.**

G53 Δός μοι ποῦ στῶ, καὶ κινῶ τὴν γῆν. *(Archimedes).* **Give me where I may stand and I will move the earth.**

G54 Μηδὲν ἄγαν. *(Solon as quoted by Diogenes Laertius, I. 63).* **Nothing too much.**

G55 Τέκνον, ἢ ταύταν ἢ ἐπὶ ταύτας. *(Plutarch, Moralia, 241 F).* **Son, come home with your shield or on it.**

G56 Τέχνη δ' ἀνάγκης ἀσθενεστέρα μακρῷ. *(Aeschylus, Prometheus, 514).* **Art is weaker far than need.**

G57 Πάντα ῥεῖ. *(Heraclitus).* **All is flux.**

G58   Σκαιὸν τὸ πλουτεῖν κἄλλο μηδὲν εἰδέναι. *(Euripides, fragment).* **Wealth without knowledge makes a boor.**

G59   Ἀρχὴ ἄνδρα δείκνυσιν. *(Bias, as quoted by Demosthenes, 1455, 15).* **Power proves the man.**

G60   Ἕλληνες ὄντες βαρβάροις δουλεύσομεν; *(Euripides, fragment).* **Shall Greeks be slaves to barbarians?**

G61   Οὐκ ἀνδρὸς ὅρκοι πίστις, ἀλλ' ὅρκων ἀνήρ. *(Aeschylus, fragment).* **It is not the oath but the man that counts.**

G62   Γνῶθι σαυτόν. *(Thales, as quoted by Diogenes Laertius).* **Know thyself.**

G63   Πρὸς κέντρα μὴ λάκτιζε. *(Aeschylus, Agamemnon, 1624).* **Kick not against the pricks.**

G64   Ἃ δ' ἂν μάθῃ παῖς, ταῦτα σῴζεσθαι φιλεῖ πρὸς γῆρας. *(Euripides, Supplices, 916-917).* **What you learn as a boy, you will likely keep to old age.**

G65   Δεινὸν δ' ἐστὶν ἡ μὴ 'μπειρία. *(Aristophanes, Ecclesiazusae, 115).* **A fearful thing is inexperience.**